A BASIC GUIDE TO

Equestrian

An Official U.S. Olympic Committee Sports Series

The U.S. Olympic Committee

Griffin Publishing Group

ISBN 1-58000-073-8

10 9 8 7 6 5 4 3 2 1

Printed in the United States of America

Editorial Statement
In the interest of brevity, the Editors have chosen to use the standard English form of address. Please be advised that this usage is not meant to suggest a restriction to, nor an endorsement of, any individual or group of individuals, either by age, gender, or athletic ability. The Editors certainly acknowledge that boys and girls, men and women, of every age and physical condition are actively involved in sports, and we encourage everyone to enjoy the sports of his or her choice.

Griffin Publishing Group
2908 Oregon Court, Suite I-5
Torrance, CA 90503
Tel: (310)381-0485 Fax: (310)381-0499

ACKNOWLEDGMENTS

PUBLISHER   Griffin Publishing Group
DIR. / OPERATIONS   Robin L. Howland
PROJECT MANAGER   Bryan K. Howland
WRITERS   Joey Parker/Suzanne Ledeboer
BOOK DESIGN   m2design group

USOC
CHAIRMAN/PRESIDENT   William J. Hybl

USET   United States Equestrian Team, Inc.
CHAIRMAN AND PRESIDENT Finn M.W. Caspersen

EDITORS   Geoffrey M. Horn
                           Catherine Gardner
PHOTOS   Hagerty Photography
                           U.S. Dressage Federation
                           U.S. Pony Clubs, Inc.
                           American Grandprix Association
                           North American Riding for the
                           Handicapped Association, Inc.
                           Miller's Harness Co.
                           State Line Tack, Inc.
SPECIAL THANKS   USET for the athlete biographical
                           information
                           American Horse Shows Associations
COVER DESIGN   m2design group
COVER PHOTO   Charles Mann
ATHLETE ON COVER   David O'Connor

Griffin Publishing Group wishes to thank the American Medical Association, the American Dental Association, Edward L. Garr, M.D., and Ray Padilla, D.D.S., for their contributions.

The United States Olympic Committee

The U.S. Olympic Committee (USOC) is the custodian of the U.S. Olympic Movement and is dedicated to providing opportunities for American athletes of all ages.

The USOC, a streamlined organization of member organizations, is the moving force for support of sports in the United States that are on the program of the Olympic and/or Pan American Games, or those wishing to be included.

The USOC has been recognized by the International Olympic Committee since 1894 as the sole agency in the United States whose mission involves training, entering, and underwriting the full expenses for the United States teams in the Olympic and Pan American Games. The USOC also supports the bid of U.S. cities to host the winter and summer Olympic Games, or the winter and summer Pan American Games, and after reviewing all the candidates, votes on and may endorse one city per event as the U.S. bid city. The USOC also approves the U.S. trial sites for the Olympic and Pan American Games team selections.

WELCOME TO THE OLYMPIC SPORTS SERIES

We feel this unique series will encourage parents, athletes of all ages, and novices who are thinking about a sport for the first time to get involved with the challenging and rewarding world of Olympic sports.

This series of Olympic sport books covers both summer and winter sports, features Olympic history and basic sports fundamentals, and encourages family involvement. Each book includes information on how to get started in a particular sport, including equipment and clothing; rules of the game; health and fitness; basic first aid; and guidelines for spectators. Of special interest is the information on opportunities for senior citizens, volunteers, and physically challenged athletes. In addition, each book is enhanced by photographs and illustrations and a complete, easy-to-understand glossary.

Because this family-oriented series neither assumes nor requires prior knowledge of a particular sport, it can be enjoyed by all age groups. Regardless of anyone's level of sports knowledge, playing experience, or athletic ability, this official U.S. Olympic Committee Sports Series will encourage understanding and participation in sports and fitness.

The purchase of these books will assist the U.S. Olympic Team. This series supports the Olympic mission and serves importantly to enhance participation in the Olympic and Pan American Games.

United States Olympic Committee

Contents

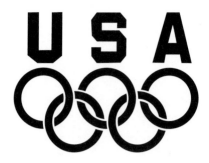

AN ATHLETE'S CREED

The most important thing in the Olympic Games is not to win but to take part, just as the most important thing in life is not the triumph but the struggle. The essential thing is not to have conquered but to have fought well.

These famous words, commonly referred to as the Olympic Creed, were once spoken by Baron Pierre de Coubertin, founder of the modern Olympic Games. Whatever their origins, they aptly describe the theme behind each and every Olympic competition.

Metric Equivalents

Wherever possible, measurements given are those specified by the Olympic rules. Other measurements are given in metric or standard U.S. units, as appropriate. For purposes of comparison, the following rough equivalents may be used.

1 kilometer (km)	= 0.62 mile (mi)	1 mi = 1.61 km
1 meter (m)	= 3.28 feet (ft)	1 ft = 0.305 m
	= 1.09 yards (yd)	1 yd = 0.91 m
1 centimeter (cm)	= 0.39 inch (in)	1 in = 2.54 cm
	= 0.1 hand	1 hand (4 in) = 10.2 cm
1 kilogram (kg)	= 2.2 pounds (lb)	1 lb = 0.45 kg
1 milliliter (ml)	= 0.03 fluid ounce (fl oz)	1 fl oz = 29.573 ml
1 liter	= 0.26 gallons (gal)	1 gal = 3.785 liters

1

Equestrian in the Olympic Games

The relationship between horses and humans covers thousands of years, from prehistory to the present. Archaeologists know that there were horse-type animals living over sixty million years ago, but we would not recognize them as horses today with their almost camel-like heads and small size. By three to four million years ago, they had become quite similar in appearance to the modern-day horse.

Prehistoric Evidence

Perhaps two million years ago in the Americas, wild horses were hunted by nomadic tribes for food and milk, but they disappeared and were not reintroduced until the time of Columbus, Cortés, and Pizarro in the fifteenth and sixteenth centuries.

Cave paintings in several areas of Europe depict Old Stone Age (3000 B.C.) horses, and archaeologists believe that this cave art, along with artifacts, shows that horses were domesticated by humans at some time. However, no one has yet determined exactly when that event occurred. The Scandinavians drove chariots pulled by pairs of small horses, and it is believed that the Lapps—expert at riding reindeer—hunted and tamed wild horses to use for riding on or pulling a sleigh in winter or a *travois* (a type of sled) in summer. A 1600 B.C. drawing from the Egyptian tomb of Harmhab shows a horseback rider, and later evidence shows hunters in Assyria and Persia (today's Iran). Rich Greeks rode horses in parades and used them for travel, while rich Romans had horse-drawn chariots and also raced them. The Romans were such good organizers and road builders that they developed messenger and transportation services using horses to bind their empire.

Historic Evidence

Recent written history has supplied rich details of the use of horses in vast areas of the world. In the far reaches of Asia—Mongolia, Manchuria, Northern India, and Siberia—animal and man joined and gained far greater range and influence with the use of a saddle, bridle, and reins. Alexander the Great and then the thirteenth-century Mongols changed the way in which wars were fought and peoples conquered. Marco Polo, the Venetian merchant and adventurer, used horses in his travels and became a conduit of not just goods but culture as well. (Using horses to transport merchandise over land was much faster than by sea.)

Medieval knights on mounted horses are symbolic of the Age of Chivalry, when tournaments were held to show the knights' skills in riding and the use of weapons. They used stirrups, probably a Chinese invention, along with a saddle, and that made riding a more effective method of controlling a horse. Renaissance man turned riding into an art form as important to his education as any of the traditional classics. But it is in the domestic arena where horses have made their most lasting contributions.

By the late eighteenth century, horses had become the power for farm equipment and were trained to control large herds of animals. When mounted, horses were a way to chase after and capture part of a person's food supply, and they also gave to man the speed and ability to cover long distances in less time. In

United States history, although stagecoaches and Pony Express riders linked villages, towns, and cities, the widespread industrialization and mechanization of the ninteenth and twentieth centuries caused a decline in the use of horses for power, but an upswing in the use of horses for the pleasure of riding. One consequence of pleasure riding was equestrian games as an Olympic sport.

For many sports, international competition was established with the arrival of the modern Olympics in 1896. But equestrian games, those involving horses, did not appear in Olympic competition until 1912, when the Olympic Games took place in Stockholm, Sweden.

In 1906, Count Clarence von Rosen, a well-traveled and highly accomplished horseman who carried the designation of "Master of the Horse" in Sweden, saw Olympic equestrian competition as a means of improving and promoting horsemanship worldwide. In a proposal to the International Olympic Committee (IOC) in 1907, von Rosen requested that equestrian events be included in upcoming Olympiads. In fact, he wanted the equestrian competition to begin as soon as the 1908 Olympics in London.

The IOC agreed. Equestrian events were added to the program and announcements were sent. Unfortunately, no one anticipated the enthusiasm with which this news would be met. The Committee thought perhaps 24-30 horses would be registered for competition and planned accordingly. So when 88 horses from eight nations appeared, it stunned the IOC. No one had anticipated such a response, and there simply wasn't any place available to stable and exercise that many horses. An equally pressing problem was that each nation had its own idea as to how the events should be judged. With so much commotion, the IOC felt it had no other choice but to cancel the equestrian competition.

Although it seemed the horses had made the long trip for nothing, the high level of interest convinced Count von Rosen that competitors and spectators alike wanted international equestrian events. Far from giving up, he immediately went to work planning an equestrian competition for the 1912 Olympics.

In 1909 von Rosen formed an international committee to select which equestrian events would be included and to establish a uniform standard of judging. One of the members of the committee was Prince Carl of Sweden, himself an avid horseman and host of the upcoming Games. Prince Carl acted as spokesman for the committee and encouraged other nations to support the establishment of equestrian events in Olympic competition. With the help of Prince Carl, von Rosen's committee was successful, and equestrian events made their long-awaited Olympic debut in the 1912 Stockholm Games.

International competition was still in its infancy, however, and the high cost of transporting horses around the world prevented many European countries from sending teams to the 1932 Games in Los Angeles. Equestrian competitions were halted during World War II, and for a few years it appeared as though von Rosen's efforts were destined to fail. After the war, however, the Olympic Games resumed with renewed vigor in 1948, and equestrian events were once again part of the program. Since then, Olympic equestrian events have grown in participation and popularity.

Entries for the equestrian games originally came from military cavalry units. But those military entries have since been replaced by civilian ones. Moreover, for many years only men rode in Olympic equestrian events; in 1952, however, Marjorie B. Haynes became the first female member of the United States Equestrian Team and represented her country at the Olympic Games in Helsinki, Finland. That same year another woman rider, Lis Hartel of Denmark, won the individual silver medal in dressage, an equestrian event that tests the ability of horse and rider to work well together. Today, almost half of the riders competing in international competitions are women. Furthermore, men and women ride together as teammates, and also compete against each other as equals.

Modern Olympic equestrian competition consists of three separate disciplines: dressage, three-day eventing, and show jumping. In each discipline, medals are awarded for both team and individual achievement. Although there have been minor changes in the format over the years, these are the same three disciplines originally selected by Count von Rosen for the 1912 Olympics.

Dressage

The origin of this type of classical training for horses can be traced to Greece in the fourth and third centuries B.C. To those ancient Greeks, the systematic training of their horses was both an artistic accomplishment and a means of improving the performance of their cavalry. The Greeks correctly realized that an easily controlled horse, one responsive to his rider's every wish, would be the most valuable type of horse a soldier could ride. If a trooper was mounted on a horse he could not control, he was of no help at all to his fellow soldiers. Therefore, with an eye toward improving the cavalry, Greek horsemen went to work devising a systematic approach to horse management.

The foundation of equitation—the act and art of horseback riding—was laid down by Xenophon, a Greek born in Athens in 430 B.C. He was a Spartan cavalry officer who trained his horses to change pace, to change direction, and to turn and circle. His horses learned to jump, were hunters, and served as cross-country mounts. Perhaps Xenophon's greatest contributions to equestrianism came from the philosophy he developed for training horses. He was patient and did not use force; he used positive reinforcement for good behavior and a light touch for disobedience. General Xenophon wrote two of the earliest known books on horse training. In this modern world of constant change, it's interesting to note that much of Xenophon's theory on riding and training horses is as accurate and valuable now as it was in his own time. Today, Xenophon's style of classical riding and training is called dressage.

Dressage is actually a French word, and was not widely used to describe classical horse training until the early eighteenth century. It is derived from the French verb *dresser*, which means "to train or to adjust." The ultimate goal of dressage training is to produce a horse that works in perfect harmony with its rider.

One world-famous example of dressage riding is found at the Spanish Riding School in Vienna, Austria. For four centuries, their Lipizzaner horses have set the standard for dressage and have traveled the world to demonstrate this classical riding style.

Xenophon, a Greek cavalry officer, laid the foundations of classical dressage. His teachings are still applicable today.

Dressage competitions are a test of both horse and rider, and the purpose is to assess the unity of the two. Horse and rider, ideally, work in harmony. In the Olympics, competitors must ride the

Grand Prix, the Grand Prix Special, and the Grand Prix Level Freestyle—the most advanced international tests. All riders are given the same amount of time to complete the same test. The tests require that riders and their horses do a prescribed variety of movements and figures. They are rigorous and include four levels of walking, trotting, and cantering, plus changes of direction, the half-halt, and transitions. All these tests are performed silently! Judges want to see a horse with free, light, and easy movements that give the impression of doing on his own what his rider requires. Needless to say, training and dedication are required from both horse and rider.

> *Grand Prix.* All team and individual competitors compete, executing 38 moves in 7 to 7 1/2 minutes. They do this from memory and are awarded points from zero to 10. Very difficult moves performed exceptionally well may receive double points.
>
> *Grand Prix Special.* This is limited and compulsory for the 25 best riders and their horses from the Grand Prix. It involves 32 movements ridden from memory.
>
> *Grand Prix Level Freestyle.* Limited to and compulsory for overall best 15 riders/horses from the Grand Prix and Grand Prix Special.

Points to Look For

If you are interested in finding a horse suitable for dressage, these are some things you should look for. A well-trained horse should be energetic and show a keen interest in its work, yet be under the rider's control and willing to carry out the rider's commands without resistance. The horse should move along with active, energetic steps, yet it should not "jig" or show other signs of disobedience. The hind legs should step well under the body, and the back should be slightly rounded in a convex (never concave) fashion to accept the rider's

Photo: Jackson Shirley for USDF

Carol Lavell riding Gifted at the
1990 World Equestrian Games in Stockholm, Sweden

weight. The neck should be long and arched with the head carried perpendicular to the ground. Almost any breed of horse can be trained in dressage; however, the larger European breeds, such as the German Hanoverian or Swedish Warmblood, are especially popular and well-suited for this discipline.

Three-Day Eventing

Many equine enthusiasts consider three-day eventing the complete test for horse and rider, as it covers all aspects of horsemanship and training: obedience and calmness in the dressage phase; boldness and speed cross-country in the endurance phase; and stamina in the stadium jumping phase. A rider must ride the same horse in all phases of the three-day event. At the Olympic Summer Games, there are two three-day eventing competitions—a team competition and an individual competition.

Phase 1

The dressage test is held the first day. The objective of the dressage test is to demonstrate the harmonious development between horse and rider. This is a difficult phase of the three-day event, in part because event horses are exceptionally keen, athletic individuals, eager to get going on the cross-country course. It is the rider's objective to demonstrate that although his horse is fit and ready to gallop and jump cross-country, the horse is still obedient and willing to perform the intricate maneuvers of the dressage test without showing resistance or impatience. Moreover, a good dressage score puts a rider among the leaders and gives him a decided advantage going into the second phase of the competition.

Photo: V. J. Zabek for USCTA

Heather Koehler prepares for combined training competition.

Phase 2

The endurance phase is held on the second day. The aim is to show not only endurance but also speed and jumping ability. The rider must demonstrate knowledge of timing and the ability to control the horse's pace. Penalties are incurred for falls or refusals to negotiate the obstacles, for going off the course, and for exceeding the time allowed.

The endurance competition has four parts: A) roads and tracks; B) steeplechase; C) roads and tracks again; and D) cross-country. Each part is assigned a "time allowed," meaning the rider's goal is to complete that part of the competition within the required time, yet without overexerting the horse. Timing is very important in the endurance phase. The rider does not want to ask more of the horse than is absolutely necessary in each part, so that the horse will have enough energy left to complete the entire competition.

Veterinarians check the horses at regular intervals, and if a veterinarian feels a horse is getting too tired, he can order the rider to give the horse a rest period of a designated length. If the horse still is not ready to continue or if the veterinarian feels a horse is unfit, he can withdraw that animal from the competition. As you can see, it is very important for a rider to practice timing and pace control to be able to make the best use of the horse's energy and ability.

Phase 3

The stadium jumping phase is held on the third and final day. Unlike the endurance part, this phase of the competition is held inside an arena, hence the term "stadium jumping." The objective is to test the horse's ability to bounce back after the endurance competition. It is not a style test, but it is difficult and shows the rider's knowledge of pace and the horse's ability to jump the 10 to 12 fences. Many times riders are tied in points at the end of the dressage and endurance phases, so the stadium jumping phase ultimately decides the winner.

Points to Look For

If you are interested in finding a horse suitable for three-day eventing, these are some points you should look for. A three-day event horse must be sound, healthy, and strong. Almost any breed of horse can be used, but the long-striding Thoroughbreds are among those most preferred. This is because of their naturally high endurance levels, their natural jumping ability, their all-around athleticism, and their ability to cover ground. A horse for this discipline must be obedient, not only to score well on the dressage test, but, even more important, to be safe to ride and jump in the endurance and stadium jumping phases of the competition. Finally, the horse must move freely forward and jump willingly. A horse that has to be coaxed over every obstacle is not going to make it as a three-day event competitor.

Show Jumping

Show jumping is one of the most crowd-pleasing of all equestrian disciplines. Far from the subjective, analytical judging used in dressage, show jumping is judged objectively—that is, the horse either clears the obstacle and completes the course within the time allowed, or it doesn't. Of course, there are a few more technicalities, but that is the essential ingredient for scoring show jumping. Because of that objective approach, even first-time horse show attendees can quickly understand what is happening on the field.

In show jumping, the horse's athletic ability and the rider's skill are tested over a course of obstacles. A competitor accumulates penalty points, called *faults*, for errors such as knocking down an obstacle, getting a hoof in the water, and/or failing to jump an obstacle. Moreover, the course must be completed within a designated period. The object is to complete the course as quickly as possible without accruing any faults.

Before the start of a show jumping competition, each rider is permitted to walk the course on foot and inspect each fence. What a rider learns about a course during this inspection walk becomes an important part of his or her strategy. The rider will

Photo: AGA

American Katie Prudent is a three-time American GrandPrix Association Rider of the Year.

determine the best location for a turn or the best possible approach to clearing a particular obstacle.

Once the inspection walk has been completed, no one is allowed on the course again until the competition begins. When the show begins, only mounted competitors, performing in their designated order, are allowed in the arena.

Each entry is assigned a number. The numbers are put into a hat, and the starting order is determined by a draw. When a rider's number is called, he or she enters the arena already mounted. The rider is not allowed to cross the starting line until the judge gives the starting signal.

In some competitions, the first round is not judged against the clock but is used as an elimination round. Only competitors with a no-fault first round are allowed to continue. Subsequent rounds *are* judged against the clock, meaning that time as well as faults will determine the winner.

Points to Look For

If you're interested in buying a show jumper, look for a horse with tremendous athletic ability, especially in lengthening or shortening its stride. Jumpers have to be able to make microsecond adjustments in their approach to an obstacle, so a horse with a smooth, "elastic" stride is essential. Also, a jumper must be responsive to the rider's every command. A horse that ignores its rider and simply plows ahead won't be able to make the tight turns found on today's highly technical jumper courses.

Almost any breed of horse can jump a few small fences, but for advanced show jumping competitions such as the Olympics and the World Cup, Thoroughbreds and Warmbloods are most often used. Their natural athletic ability is well-suited for Grand Prix jumping.

Photo: Hagerty Photo

Mary Slouka, jumping a course obstacle

Gate

Hog's back

Rustic

Brush

Triple

Painted panel and poles

Chicken coop

Post and rail

Course obstacles

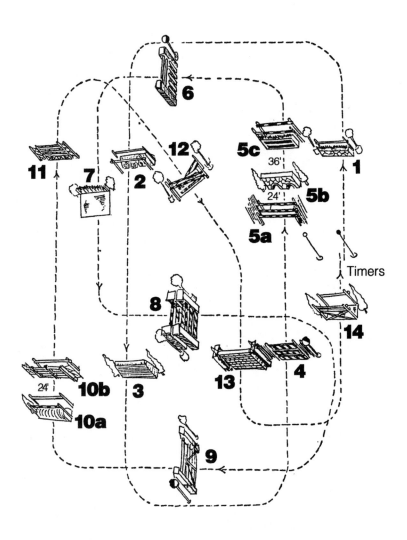

24' means two strides between 5a and 5b and between 10a and 10b; 36' means three strides between 5b and 5c.

Today's Grand Prix courses require very advanced riding skills.

Jumps on Grand Prix Course

1. Brush and rails

2. Chicken coop and rails

3. Vertical wall

4. Vertical planks

5. First combination on the course—

      5a. Three-rail spread

      5b. Stone wall

      5c. Brush and rails

6. Gate and rails

7. Water jump

8. Rails over planks

9. Vertical gate

10. Second combination on the course—

      10a. Rails over a barrel

      10b. Planks with hidden rail behind

11. Vertical planks

12. Swedish oxer

13. Vertical wall

14. Rails over a liverpool

Olympic Medal Highlights, 1912-1996

Since the 1912 Games, the United States has won 41 Olympic medals in equestrian. Of that total, 30 have been won since 1952, the year the United States Equestrian Team (USET) assumed responsibility for selecting, training, and fielding American equestrian teams.

1952 Helsinki, Finland
(2) Bronze Jumping Team; Three-Day Team

1960 Rome, Italy
(1) Silver   Jumping Team

1964 Tokyo, Japan
(1) Silver   Three-Day Team

1968 Mexico City, Mexico
(1) Gold   William Steinkraus/Snowbound, Individual Jumping
(1) Silver   Three-Day Team
(1) Bronze Michael Page/Foster, Three-Day Individual

1972 Munich, West Germany
(2) Silver   Jumping Team; Three-Day Team
(1) Bronze Neal Shapiro/Sloopy, Individual Jumping

1976 Montreal, Canada
(2) Gold   Tad Coffin/Bally Cor, Individual Three-Day;
                Three-Day Team
(1) Silver   J. Michael Plumb/Better and Better, Ind. Three-Day
(1) Bronze Dressage Team

1980 Alternate Games, Rotterdam, Holland
(1)Bronze   Melanie Smith/Calypso, Individual Jumping

1980 Alternate Games, Fontainebleau, France
(1) Silver   James Wofford/Catawich, Individual Three-Day
(1) Bronze Torrance Watkins/Poltroon, Individual Three-Day

1984 Los Angeles, United States
(3) Gold   Joe Fargis/Touch of Class, Individual Jumping,
                Three-Day Team; Jumping Team,
(2) Silver   Conrad Homfeld/Abdullah, Individual Jumping;
                Karen Stives/Ben Arthur, Individual Three-Day

1988 Seoul, South Korea
(2) Silver   Greg Best/Gem Twist, Individual Jumping;
                Jumping Team

1992 Barcelona, Spain
(2) Bronze Norman Dello Joio/Irish, Individual Jumping;
                Dressage Team

1996 Atlanta, United States
(2) Silver   Three-Day Team, Jumping Team
(2) Bronze Kerry Millikan/Landlady, Individual Three-Day
                Dressage Team

Meet the U.S. Teams

DRESSAGE TEAM

©2000 Charles Mann

BLINKS, SUSAN

Hometown: Wellington, FL

Birthdate: October 5, 1957

Horse: Flim Flam—Bay gelding, 16.1 hands, 11 years old, Hanoverian

Delano—Dark brown gelding, 16.3 hands, 13 years old, Dutch

Owner: Dressage Sponsor Corporation

Susan Blinks qualified for the 2000 Olympic Games in Sydney, Australia, by winning the State Line Tack/USET Dressage Championship, presented by Rio Suite Hotel and Casino in

Loxahatchee, FL. Blinks was a member of the fourth place USET squad at the 1998 World Equestrian Games in Rome, Italy. She also rode Flim Flam to an individual twelfth place finish. Later in the year she was named 1998 USOC Female Equestrian Athlete of the Year. A 1997 USET Training and Competition grant recipient, she earned a Team Gold Medal at the 1997 CDIO Hickstead in England and rode Flim Flam to a first place finish in the Grand Prix Special. She also finished second and third (aboard Flim Flam and Delano respectively) in the Miller's/USET Grand Prix Championship presented by Rio Suite Hotel and Casino. She earned high honors with second and third place finishes in the Grand Prix, Special, and Freestyle at the 1997 Bayer/USET Festival of Champions.

Blinks also rode to numerous victories on the 1997 Florida dressage circuit. She won the Grand Prix and Special at Wellington, and the Grand Prix qualifier and Freestyle at the Winter Equestrian Festival Dressage Classic in Florida. She also won the Grand Prix and Intermediaire II at the Gold Coast Opener and the Special at the Florida Dressage Classic.

Blinks won the 1996 Grand Prix Special at the CDI-W New England Dressage Association aboard Flim Flam. At the Royal Dressage Festival in New York, she was victorious in the USET Grand Prix Special qualifier and the Intermediaire II. In 1989, Blinks was long-listed for the North American Championships. As a teen, Blinks trained with Marianne Ludwig. After graduating from the University of Massachusetts, she trained with Walter Christenson in Germany. Blinks then moved to New York and worked briefly with Robert Dover. She also trained with Mr. Schulten-Baumer for two years in Germany. Blinks is an American Horse Shows Association dressage judge. She teaches and trains out of the Kundrun Farm in Mount Kisco, NY.

COSTELLO, ROBERT

Hometown: Southern Pines, NC

Birthdate: July 26, 1965

Horse: Chevalier—Chestnut Thoroughbred gelding, 16.2 hands, 1989

Owner: Deirdre Pirie

©2000 Charles Mann

A native of South Hamilton, MA, Robert Costello took the reins of Chevalier for the owner Deirdre Pirie ofter the horse's former rider, Pirie's daughter Amanda Warrington, died tragically. Costello has had great success with the horse, highlighted by top-ten finishes in the USET Fall Championship at the Fair Hill CCI*** in October 1999 and the USET Four-Star Championship at Rolex Kentucky Three Day Event CCI**** in April 2000. Robert also competes in Show Jumping and Eventing.

DOVER, ROBERT

Hometown: Flemington, NJ

Birthdate: June 7, 1956

Horse: Rainier—Gray Oldenburg gelding, 17.0 hands, 1991

Owner: Jane F. Clark

©2000 Charles Mann

Robert Dover has won more dressage honors than any other American competitor. He is a veteran of four Olympics (1984, 1988, 1992, and 1996), winning team Bronze Medals in 1992 and 1996. He was also a World Championship team Bronze Medalist in 1994.

Dover had the highest finish ever by an American (fourth) at the 1988 World Cup Final and he is a five-time USET Dressage Champion.   In 1994 he was awarded the U.S. Olympic Committee's Male Equestrian Athlete of the Year award. Dover had a string of 1994 achievements which included being awarded the USET's Whitney Stone Cup for his distinguished record in international competition. Riding Devereaux he had Grand Prix and Freestyle wins in the U.S. League Final for the Dressage World Cup.   He finished fifth at the World Equestrian Games Grand Prix Freestyle in Holland and helped the USET win a team Bronze Medal.

In 1992 he was the leading qualifier for the Olympic selection trial on Lectron, whom he'd been riding for just a few months. Dover played a key role in helping the USET win a team Bronze Medal that year at the Olympic Games in Barcelona. He also represented the United States in the 1990 World Equestrian Games. In 1989 Dover led his teammates to the team Gold Medal at the North American Dressage Championship in Quebec, Canada, while capturing the individual Silver Medal. In 1988 he was the highest placed American rider at the Olympic Games in Seoul with Federlicht. Dover spent 1987 competing in Europe with the horses Federlicht and Juvel. His many successes there included winning the Grand Prix Freestyle in Aachen, as well as wins in Rotterdam, Hannover, and Zuidlaren. He was also Leading Rider at Hannover and Brussels.

He credits his success to the late Colonel Bengt Ljungquist, his trainer for many years. He also trained with Herbert Rehbien of Germany.

©2000 Charles Mann

RAINE, KATHLEEN

Hometown: Laguna Hills, CA

Birthdate: July 19, 1965

Horse: Fidelia—Bay (Dutch) Warmblood mare, 16.2 hands, 1987

Owner: Kathleen Raine

Kathleen Raine placed third in the State Line Tack/USET Dressage Championship, presented by Rio Suite Hotel and Casino in Loxahatchee, FL, helping earn her a spot on the 2000 U.S. Olympic team. Raine helped the USET win the team Bronze Medal for the Dressage World Championship at the 1994 World Equestrian Games in Holland. She was the U.S. League Final Reserve Champion in 1994 and finished sixth overall at the Dressage World Cup Final in Gothenburg, Sweden. While competing abroad in 1995, Raine was also a team Bronze Medalist at Rotterdam and finished first in the Grand Prix Freestyle at CDI Donaueschingen.

On U.S. soil, Raine has added many impressive wins to her career accomplishments. In 1999 she won the Grand Prix at Dressage at Indio I. In 1996 she won the Miller's/USET Grand Prix qualifier at Del Mar Dressage and Los Angeles CDI. In 1995 she was also victorious in both the Grand Prix and Freestyle at Paddock CDI-W. In addition, she won the Grand Prix Freestyle at DG Bar Ranch Show and the Grand Prix Special at CDI-W Flintridge.

Raine began competing in dressage after graduating from high school and has been coached by Olympic veteran Hilda Gurney, Johann Hinnemann, and Dennis Callin. She resides in Rolling Hills, CA, with her husband David Wightman, who also competes in dressage.

©2000 Charles Mann

SEIDEL, GUENTER

Hometown: Del Mar, CA

Birthdate: September 23, 1960

Horse: Foltaire—Bay gelding, 16.2 hands, 11 years old, Dutch

Owner: Dick and Jane Brown

German native Guenter Seidel qualified for the 2000 Sydney Olympic Games by placing second on Foltaire in the State Line Tack/USET Dressage Championship, presented by Rio Suite Hotel and Casino in Loxahatchee, FL. Seidel rode Graf George to a team Bronze Medal at the 1996 Atlanta Olympic Games. He also placed eighth individually, finishing seventh in the Grand Prix Freestyle and tenth in the Grand Prix Special. Seidel won the 1998 Miller's/USET Dressage Championship after his performance at the Bayer/USET Festival of Champions. Later in the year, at the World Equestrian Games, Seidel was a member of the fourth place USET squad and finished ninth overall in the World Dressage Championships. In 1997 Seidel won the Grand Prix and Special at the German National Horse Show in Germany. He also placed eighth overall at that year's World Cup Final in 's-Hertogenbosch, The Netherlands.

Seidel, riding three horses, produced great results in his quest for a spot on the 1996 Olympic Team. He rode Graf George and Numir into the top 12 during the Olympic Trials, and Tanzen finished 17th. Seidel won the Intermediaire I Championship aboard D'Artagnon, and finished third with Foltaire. He also won the U.S. League Final for the Volvo World Cup, and Los Angeles' Mid-Winter CDI-W Grand Prix and Special. In 1995 Seidel won a team Silver Medal at the Pan American Games and a team Gold Medal at the Can-Am Dressage Challenge. He was a Bronze Medalist at the 1994 U.S. Olympic Festival and won the 1992 Miller's/USET Intermediaire I Championship aboard Numir.

Prior to coming to the United States in 1985, Seidel received his Bereiter degree in Germany. Today he rides full-time and teaches and trains dressage riders and horses.

©2000 Charles Mann

TRAURIG, CHRISTINE

Hometown: Carlsbad, CA

Birthdate: March 13, 1957

Horse: Etienne—Dark bay Westphalian gelding, 18.0 hands, 1988

Owner: Mr. and Mrs. Robert Haas

Christine Traurig earned a place on the U.S. Olympic Dressage Team by placing fourth in the State Line/USET Dressage Championship in Loxahatchee, FL, on Mr. and Mrs. Robert Haas' Etienne. Traurig made her return to dressage competition in 1997 after a four-year absence from the sport. She turned in a solid performance at the 1997 Bayer/USET Festival of Champions, finishing eighth overall in the Miller's/USET Grand Prix Championship presented by Rio Suite Hotel and Casino. She also rode Assini Boin to a fifth place finish in the Grand Prix Special. Earlier in 1997, she won the USET Grand Prix qualifier and the Grand Prix Special at The Paddock Spring Festival of Dressage in Los Angeles.

Traurig was born and raised in the Hanover area of Germany.

SHOW JUMPING TEAM

©2000 Charles Mann

GARSON, NONA

Hometown: Lebanon, NJ

Birthdate: September 30, 1959

Horse: Rhythmical—Chestnut Russian gelding, 15.3 hands, 1985

Owner: The Kamine Family and Nona Garson

Nona Garson was a recipient of a U.S. Equestrian Team (USET) grant to represent the U.S. on a 1997 European tour where her double clear ride helped the USET win the Nations' Cup at Rotterdam. She was one of 12 riders to contribute to the USET's win in the inaugural Samsung Nations' Cup Series in 1997. She started 1998 with a win on Rhythmical in the $50,000 Cosequin Grand Prix of Palm Beach, one of three Grand Prix wins she had in 1998, a year which saw her ride for the USET in the Show Jumping World Championships at the World Equestrian Games in Rome.

Garson began riding at the age of five in New Jersey. As a junior, she rose through the equitation ranks. With her father, George, Garson established the Ridge Farm, which she now owns and operates while training with George Morris. In 1995 Garson won her first Grand Prix in the final Pan American Games selection trial at W. Palm Beach, FL. She then was a member of the Bronze Medal-winning USET squad at the Pan American Games in Buenos Aires, Argentina. She captured the Leading Lady Rider award in La Baule, France, that same year. She and Rhythmical won the Budweiser/American GrandPrix Association

Championship in February 1999 and followed that with a win in the $100,000 Jaguar Gold Coast Grand Prix one month later.

©2000 Charles Mann

GOLDSTEIN ENGLE, MARGIE

Hometown: Wellington, FL

Birthdate: March 31, 1958

Horse: Hidden Creek's Perin—Bay Westphalian gelding, 17.1 hands, 1990

Owner: Hidden Creek Farm

Adding to her impressive résumé of show jumping successes in 1999, Margie Goldstein Engle rode Hidden Creek's Alvaretto to the team Silver Medal at the Pan American Games in Winnipeg, Canada, in July, following her victory in the $150,000 Budweiser American Invitational in April. This adds to a long list of major wins. She captured the $100,000 Rolex/USET Show Jumping Championship, presented by Ethel M Chocolates at the 1998 Bayer/USET Festival of Champions. She was one of 12 riders to contribute to the U.S. Equestrian Team's win in the inaugural Samsung Nations' Cup Series in 1997. She was a recipient of a USET grant to represent the U.S. on a 1997 European tour, where she teamed with Hidden Creek's Laurel to help the USET capture Nations' Cup victories at Rome and St. Gallen; in addition, the pair won the prestigious Grand Prix of Rome. Goldstein Engle also won the Grand Prix at Arnhem, Netherlands, on Hidden Creek's Alvaretto during the tour. In February 1997, Goldstein Engle won the Budweiser/ AGA Show Jumping Championship, which clinched her a record fifth Budweiser Grand Prix Rider of the Year Award.

One of the most active riders on the Grand Prix circuit, Goldstein Engle was the American Grand Prix Association Rider of the Year for the first time in 1989. After winning the first Grand Prix of 1990, she suffered a severe riding accident that March when her mount fell and crushed bones in her leg. She returned to competition while still using crutches and gained five top-three placings before the year was out.

Leaving her injury in the past, Goldstein Engle won five AGA events in 1991 and regained her AGA Rider of the Year title; she was also named the 1991 AHSA/Hertz Equestrian of the Year. In 1992, Goldstein Engle was named the Rolex/National Grand Prix League Rider of the Year, a feat she repeated in 1993. She was named AGA Rider of the Year again in 1994 and 1995.

Goldstein Engle has set lots of records: most AGA wins with the same horse in the same season (five wins on Saluut II in 1991); most Grand Prix wins in a single season (11); and two Grand Prix wins in two days. She is the first rider to place six horses in the ribbons in a single Grand Prix class, and the first rider ever to place first, second, third, fourth, and fifth in a single Grand Prix class. In 1998 she tied for sixth place in the World Cup Final in Helsinki, Finland, and was first alternate for the USET's World Equestrian Games squad.

Goldstein Engle is a graduate of Florida International University with a degree in business education.

©2000 Charles Mann

HAAS, ELISE K.

Hometown: Sausalito, CA

Birthdate: May 22, 1979

Horse: Mr. Blue—Gray Dutch stallion, 16.2 hands, 1988

Owner: Mr. and Mrs. Robert Haas

Following an already impressive start to the 1999 season, Elise Haas won the $234,000 Grand Prix Edouard Leclec in Cannes, France, on Aphnee Du Marais. She topped an international field of 27 entries which included Olympic veterans from Great Britain, Germany, Belgium, France, Switzerland, Ireland, and Brazil.

Haas placed third in one of the nation's biggest Grand Prix events, the $150,000 Budweiser American Invitational in Tampa in April 1999. Later that summer, she was selected to take part in the USET Developing Rider Tour which traveled to Europe to compete in CSIO competitions, She and her teammates were dubbed the "Fab Four" by the European press, winning two Nations' Cups in Falsterbo, Sweden, and Budapest, Hungary, and placing second in Lummen, Belgium.

Elise Haas first received attention when she won the BET/USET Show Jumping Talent Search Finals West, presented by Sooner Trailer, in 1997. She began her Grand Prix career in 1997 and wan the Pacific Coast Horse Show Association Rookie of the Year.

Haas graduated from high school in 1996 and deferred admission to Harvard in order to pursue her career in riding.

©2000 Charles Mann

HOUGH, LAUREN

Hometown: Ocala, FL

Birthdate: April 11, 1977

Horse: Clasiko—Dark bay, German gelding, 16.3 hands, 1992

Owner: The Clasiko Group

Lauren Hough is the daughter of prominent hunter judges Linda and Champ Hough, who was on the 1952 Three-Day Event Olympic team. Through her junior years she has earned hunter championships in all major divisions. In 1993 she made her debut on the Grand Prix circuit and earned the title of Pacific Coast Horseman's Association Rookie of the Year at the age of 15. Lauren earned a second place finish in the 1997 $25,000 Ariat Challenge Cup Round II in Wellington, FL. In 1998, with several top 10 finishes on the Florida circuit, Lauren placed fourth with Picasso in the $50,000 Four Points Inn Grand Prix of Tampa-CSI-W. In only her second appearance, Lauren placed fifth with Picasso in the $100,000 Budweiser American Invitational. Although showing only on a few occasions during the summer, she and Picasso earned a win at the $25,000 New Hope Welcome Class.

In 2000, Lauren placed ninth in the $100,000 Rolex/U.S. Show Jumping Championship, presented by the AHSA and the USET, to advance her to the final U.S. Olympic Selection Trials in California. Lauren is an active trainer with several talented students.

©2000 Charles Mann

KRAUT, LAURA

Hometown: Oconomowoc, WI

Birthdate: November 14, 1965

Horse: Liberty—Bay Dutch Warmblood mare, 16.2 hands, 1991

Owner: Summit Group

Formerly from Camden, SC, Laura began riding at the age of three in Atlanta, GA, with her mother, Carol Kent. After an injury in 1988 forced her to take a brief respite from competition, Laura returned with a vengeance later in the year to tie an AGA record by placing first, second, and third at the $30,000 Cadillac Grand Prix of Houston. Later in the season, she piloted Benny Hill and Ruebens to a one-two finish in the $30,000 Milwaukee Classic. She earned a team Silver and individual Bronze medal at the 1989 U.S. Olympic Festival. In 1992 aboard Simba Run she was named as first alternate for the Olympic Games held in Barcelona. In 1993 Laura and Simba Run placed 12 times nationally and won the $30,000 Mednikow Germantown Grand Prix. In 1994 the pair placed eighth in the $125,000 Budweiser/AGA Championships during the Winter Equestrian Festival and qualified for the Volvo World Cup Finals in 's-Hertogenbosch, Netherlands, where she finished 35th overall.

For 1996 Laura and longtime partner Simba Run won the $30,000 Grand Prix of Indianapolis, and in 1997 the pair captured the $30,000 Kentucky Spring Classic. With mounts Classified and Sunday II, Laura won the $30,000 Motor City Grand Prix in June and the $30,000 Turfway Park Grand Prix in July. The year 1998 saw Laura in the winner's circle on two occasions—first at the $50,000 Sweet Charity Grand Prix (IN) with Athletico and next in the $87,462 Queen Elizabeth Cup in Calgary, Canada, with Simba Run.

Her 1999 season included several top placings with her old friend Simba Run, in addition to solid ribbons with her more recent partner, Liberty. Kraut imported the Dutch Warmblood from the Netherlands in 1999 and is looking toward a bright future with the talented mare. Laura is married to amateur Grand Prix rider Bob Kraut, and they have a son born in 1999.

©2000 Charles Mann

MINIKUS, TODD

Hometown: Lake Forest, IL

Birthdate: June 11, 1962

Horse: Oh Star—Chestnut Oldenburg stallion, 16.2 hands, 1991

Owner: Todd Minikus, Ltd.

Todd Minikus was a recipient of a U.S. Equestrian Team (USET) grant to represent the U.S. on a 1997 European tour. He is a frequent visitor to the winner's circle. In recent years, he and Ravel have captured several Grand Prix wins, including the $100,000 Budweiser American Invitational in Tampa, FL, in April 1997.

Minikus began showing at the Grand Prix level in 1985. He achieved great success with his gray Canadian Thoroughbred, Thrilling. Minikus rode Thrilling to four Grand Prix wins in 1989 and then took the show jumping world by storm in 1990 with an unprecedented sweep of all open jumper classes at the Washington International Horse Show, including the President's Cup. His record-setting performance earned him Washington's Ennis Jenkins Award as Leading Rider (he was both Leading Gentleman and Leading National Rider) to go with that year's

Midwest Grand Prix Rider of the Year award. Thrilling also earned honors as Midwest Horse of the Year.

In addition to 1999's European tour, Minikus represented the U.S. in the 1991 and 1995 World Cup Finals, and on a 1996 USET European Developing Rider tour. He had five Grand Prix wins in 1998. Minikus is currently the trainer at Horse Forum Ltd. in Lake Forest, IL.

EVENTING TEAM

©2000 Charles Mann

BLACK, JULIE

Hometown: Newnan, GA

Birthdate: September 26, 1970

Horse: Hyde Park Corner—Bay Thoroughbred gelding, 16.2 hands, 1990

Owner: Jim and Janet Richards

Julie Black began riding at the age of three when her mother bought her a pony. She competed at Pony Club local shows, and became interested in cross-country. She has her B.A. degree from the University of Georgia. Outside the equestrian world Black's priorities are her family and running a successful business. Her husband, Stuart, also trains horses and competes for the Canadian Equestrian Team. She has competed in CCI's at the three-star level in both the U.S. and the U.K. and finished fifth in the Rolex/ USET CCI**** Championship at the Rolex Kentucky Three Day Event, presented by Bayer in April 1999, and third in the CCIO *** of the Pan American Games in Canada.

©2000 Charles Mann

DAVIDSON, BRUCE

Hometown: Unionville, PA

Birthdate: December 30, 1949

Horse: Squelch—Chestnut gelding, 16.0 hands, 12 years old, Thoroughbred

Heyday—Bay gelding, 16.0 hands, 11 years old, Thoroughbred Bally

Mist—Bay gelding, 16.1 hands, 6 years old, Thoroughbred

Owner: George Strawbridge and Dr. Elinor B. Jenny

A two-time World Three Day Event Champion, Bruce Davidson has been the U.S. Combined Training Association (USCTA) Rider of the Year a record 14 times. He was a member of two Gold Medal-winning U.S. Equestrian Team (USET) Olympic squads, at Montreal in 1976 and Los Angeles in 1984, as well as Silver Medal-winning teams at Munich in 1972 and Atlanta in 1996. In May 1997, Davidson won the Punchestown CCI*** Three Day Event. The year 1995 was a busy and successful one for Davidson. In March he won individual Gold and team Silver Medals at the Pan American Games. He also became the first American ever to win the Badminton CCI****, and placed second at the Checkmate CCI***.

Davidson made his USET debut riding on the 1972 Silver Medal-winning Munich Olympic Games team, placing eighth individually. He was the first American to win a Gold Medal at the World Three Day Event Championship in 1974 and led the USET to its first world title. In 1978 his defense of his World Championship Gold Medal made him the only American event rider to win two World Championships, and he helped the USET win a team Bronze Medal. His next World Championship medal, an individual Bronze, came at the first World Equestrian Games in Stockholm, Sweden, in 1990.

Raised on a farm in Millbrook, NY, Davidson left Iowa State University in 1970 after his third year of pre-veterinary medicine to train with USET Three-Day coach Jack Le Goff. Davidson is the father of two children, both of whom compete in three-day eventing.

©2000 Charles Mann

DAVIDSON, BUCK

Hometown: Unionville, PA

Birthdate: February 11, 1976

Horse: Special Attention—Bay Thoroughbred gelding, 16.3 hands, 1989

Owner: Debbie Adams and Tony Rozati

Buck Davidson, son of five-time U.S. Olympic veteran Bruce Davidson, has won the Markham Trophy as the highest placing Young Rider in a USET Championship three times. In 1997 he won individual and team Silver Medals at the North American Young Riders' Championships. In 1998 he rode in his first four- star event, placing sixth on Trans Am Aflirt at the Rolex Kentucky Three Day Event Championship, presented by Bayer. He rode Pajama Game to tenth in the Rolex Kentucky Three Star Championship in 1998 and to fourth in 1999. In 1999 he rode for the USET in the Pan American Games in Winnipeg, Canada, and finished seventh.

DOUGLAS, BECKY

©2000 Charles Mann

Hometown: Lansing, KS

Birthdate: April 24, 1969

Horse: Highland Hogan—Bay Thoroughbred gelding, 16.0 hands, 1991

Owner: Faye C. and David Woolf

In 1999, Becky Douglas and Highland Hogan placed tenth in the Advanced Horse Trials at Morven Park in Virginia, fifth at Menfelt in Maryland, and won at Wayne duPage in Illinois. They placed second in the CCI** at Camino Real in Texas and sixth in the CCI*** at the Fair Hill International in Fair Hill, MD. Douglas came in 11th at the CCI**** 2000 Rolex Kentucky Three Day Event, presented by Bayer. In 1999, Highland Hogan was Area IV overall Horse of the Year and Area V Intermediate Horse of the Year.

FOUT, NINA

©2000 Charles Mann

Hometown: Middleburg, VA

Birthdate: June 23, 1959

Horse: 3 Magic Beans—Bay Thoroughbred gelding, 17.0 hands, 1990

Owner: Nina Fout

A lifelong horsewoman, Nina Fout has risen quickly through the ranks of three-day event riders over the past four years. She went from finishing 21st in the Fair Hill CCI*** in 1995 to finishing 14th in the Punchestown CCI*** in 1997. She completed the Advanced Horse Trials at Thirleston Castle, Scotland, and finished 26th in the CCI*** at Blenheim, Great Britain. In 1998 she placed 11th in the Advanced Horse Trials at Groton House (MA) and 10th at the Millbrook (NY), on the way to a 9th in the CCI*** at Fair Hill (MD). In 1999 and 2000, Fout and 3 Magic Beans turned in successful four-star performances at Badminton (18th), Burghley (13th, top US finish) and the Rolex Kentucky Three Day Event (12th).

©2000 Charles Mann

LUFKIN, ABIGAIL

Hometown: Middleburg, VA

Birthdate: April 4, 1971

Horse: Jacob Two Two—Bay, gelding, 15.3 hands, 11 years, Thoroughbred

Hannigan—Bay Thoroughbred gelding, 16.1 hands, 1991

Owner: Team Lufkin

Abigail Lufkin, a graduate of Brown University, won the individual Bronze Medal at the 1991 Pan American Championships. She has trained with several of the sport's top instructors, including Mike Plumb and David O'Connor. She was Reserve Champion in the 1998 Rolex/USET Three-Star Spring Championship, presented by Bayer at the Rolex Kentucky Three-Day Event, and was third overall in the CCI**** Championship at the 1999 Rolex Kentucky Three Day Event presented by Bayer. She won two team Gold Medals plus individual Bronze and Silver medals at the 1987 and 1989 North

American Young Rider Championships and represented the USET at the 1998 World Three Day Event Championships at the World Equestrian Games. An all-around athlete, Lufkin also hikes, bikes, and water skis.

©2000 Charles Mann

O'CONNOR, DAVID

Hometown: The Plains, VA

Birthdate: January 18, 1962

Horse: Giltedge—Bay gelding, 12 years old, 17.0 hands, Irish Thoroughbred

Owner: Jacqueline Mars

Horse: Custom Made—Dark bay Thoroughbred gelding, 17.0 hands, 1985

Owner: Xandarius, LLC

Horse: Rattle N Hum—Dark bay Thoroughbred gelding, 16.1 hands, 1991

Owner: David Lenaburg

David O'Connor won the Mitsubishi Motors Badminton Horse Trials CCI**** in May 1997, becoming only the second American to win this event in its 49-year history. Following his return from Europe, O'Connor captured the Cosequin/USET Three Day Event Fall Championship at the Fair Hill CCI***. He and his wife, Karen, were teammates on the Silver Medal-winning U.S. Equestrian Team (USET) squad at the 1996 Atlanta Olympic Games.

O'Connor won the 1995 Rolex/Kentucky Three Day Event Spring Championship. Later that year, he became one of only three riders to capture both the spring and fall USET Championships when he won the USET Fall Three Day Event Championship at the Fair Hill International CCI***. Two years earlier, riding Wilton Fair, O'Connor won the USET Fall Championship. The win served as a fitting tribute for the veteran campaigner, Wilton Fair, who was retired from competition following his victory. O'Connor had been the highest placed American (seventh) at the 1992 Badminton CCI**** in England, aboard Wilton Fair. He was a member of the USET squad at the 1990 World Equestrian Games in Stockholm, Sweden, a position he earned after winning the Rolex/Kentucky International Three Day Event earlier that spring. That same year, he was third in the Advanced division at the Fair Hill Horse Trials in Maryland, and sixth in the Brighting Park Horse Trials in England.

O'Connor was the only one of five Americans competing to finish the course at the 1987 Burghley CCI****. He competed internationally for the USET throughout the late 1980s, beginning at the 1986 CCI*** Alternate World Championship in Bialy Bor, Poland, on Border Raider. O'Connor rode as an individual in the 1994 World Equestrian Games World Three Day Event Championship. At the 1998 World Equestrian Games in Italy, he was the highest placed American, finishing sixth, helping the United States to the team Bronze Medal.

A powerful and winning husband-and-wife team, David and Karen O'Connor divide their time between farms in the United States and England. At the 1999 Pan American in Winnipeg, Canada, David O'Connor won team Gold and individual Silver Medals, earning him August Athlete of the Month.

©2000 Charles Mann

O'CONNOR, KAREN

Hometown: The Plains, VA

Birthdate: February 17, 1958

Horse: Prince Panache—Bay Thoroughbred gelding, 17.0 hands, 1984

Owner: Jacqueline Mars

Karen (Lende) O'Connor won the Rolex Kentucky Three Day Event, CCI**** in Lexington, to start out the 1999 season. She won the team Silver Medal at the 1996 Olympic Games in Atlanta with husband and teammate, David O'Connor. She first made a World Championship team when she qualified in 1982. However, she was forced to withdraw when her horse became sick.

In 1984, riding The Optimist, O'Connor became the first American to win the Boekelo (Netherlands) CCI. Taking over fellow U.S. Equestrian Team (USET) veteran Jim Wofford's mount, Castlewellan, she won the 1985 Chesterland (PA) CCI in their first three-day event together. O'Connor was a member of the 1988 USET Olympic squad, riding The Optimist. The following year, she retired The Optimist and campaigned Nos Ecus, clinching both the Radnor and Fair Hill events, and taking the first of three consecutive U.S. Combined Training Association (USCTA) Lady Rider of the Year titles.

On the basis of her performance in 1991 with Mr. Maxwell, the USET provided a grant for O'Connor to compete in Europe. While there, she finished third at Burghley, and Mr. Maxwell was named USCTA and the *Chronicle of the Horse*'s Horse of the Year. She placed first and third in the 1993 Punchestown CCI*** Three Day Event, and third in a CCI** at Loughanmore, Ireland. Based on her international performances, the U.S.

Olympic Committee (USOC) named O'Connor its 1993 Female Equestrian Athlete of the Year. Together with David, she divides her time between the U.S. and England.

©2000 Charles Mann

WIESMAN, LINDEN

Hometown: Bluemont, VA

Birthdate: January 23, 1975

Horse: Primitive Gold—Bay gelding, 16.3 hands, 9 years old, Thoroughbred

Owner: Barbara and James Wiesman

In 1999 Wiesman and Anderoo completed the Advanced Horse Trials at Pine Top, GA, and placed fourth at Southern Pines, NC. They also placed 14th in the CCI *** at the Fair Hill International. Wiesman placed 13th on Primitive Gold at the 1999 Rolex Kentucky Three Day Event CCI ***, presented by Bayer, and sixth at Southern Pines. In 2000 they placed eighth in the Advanced Horse Trials at Sharpton III in Florida. Wiesman came in 14th at the 2000 Rolex Kentucky Three Day Event CCI ****, presented by Bayer. Wiesman won the Harry T. Peters Young Rider Championship in 1993 and 1994 and was short listed for the Pan American Games team in 1999.

3

Selecting a Riding School

No matter what your level of experience is with horses, a good riding school can be your best friend. You can take lessons from qualified instructors; you'll have access to facilities such as well-footed riding rings, bath racks, and "hot walkers"; your horse will have access to top veterinarians, as well as horseshoeing, transportation (if you go to horse shows), and training; and, perhaps most important, there will be experienced horsemen around to assist you in an emergency. You'll make friends with people who like horses just as much as you do, and you'll always have someone with whom to ride. It is especially important to have a riding buddy if you are heading out on unfamiliar trails. A good riding school can give you all of these benefits, and more.

Finding a Stable

If you are new to riding or have recently moved to a new location, you'll want to know how to find stables in your area. You can try the phone book, but most training barns don't advertise in general directories. Use the phone book to locate tack and feed stores in your area. Call or visit your neighborhood tack and feed dealer.

Tack shop owners always know where the best training barns are located and can be a gold mine of information. Write down the names and phone numbers they give you; then call each barn and make an appointment to visit. Tell the barn you would like to meet the staff during your visit and ask whether you could have a short conference with the instructor, trainer, and/or stable manager. If you just show up at the barn without calling, the instructor may be teaching a class or schooling a horse. It's not fair to expect the instructor to stop everything if that person didn't know you were coming. Call first and confirm the best time for you to visit.

If you can't find a tack or feed store in the phone book, try the office of an equine veterinarian. For professional reasons, a vet's office may be reluctant to divulge information about any particular establishment, but if you explain that you are new to horses or new to the area and you're completely lost, that office may give you the names of some barns to contact. A lot of your success depends on how politely you present yourself. Realize, too, that should the vet's office be in the middle of an emergency, the people there simply won't have time to talk to you. Don't be offended. Simply thank them, hang up, and try again in a day or two.

If none of those approaches work for you, try locating a training stable outside your immediate area. Explain your situation and see if the people there can recommend anyone closer to you. If you subscribe to any equine magazines, check the classified listings, or call the magazine and ask staff members if they know of any stables in your area. If you live near a college or university, contact the athletic department and ask if there's a riding program. If so, someone in the riding group should be able to help you.

Once you have located the stables in your area, it's up to you to arrange to visit each one, then to select the one that best meets your needs.

Benefits, Safety, and Costs

Both horse and rider benefit from being with a quality riding stable. If you own your own horse and board at the riding stable, the horse will be supervised during the hours that you cannot be there. Should your horse become ill or injured, someone will be there to tend to its immediate care and, if necessary, call the veterinarian. You will know that your horse will always have fresh water, and will be fed properly and on time. These facts alone give any responsible horse owner added peace of mind, but both horse and rider benefit in other ways as well. In a top stable you will have access to a variety of aids, such as safe, well-constructed jumps; good riding arenas; hot walkers; bath racks; cross-ties; bull pens; lettered dressage arenas; tack rooms; pasture or turnout pens; and clean feed rooms. In addition, you can take lessons from qualified instructors, and your horse will be serviced by competent professionals for all veterinary and shoeing needs. All of these things are benefits, both to you and to your horse.

The safety factor is fairly obvious: should an emergency arise, you won't be left alone to deal with a frightening or stressful situation. Moreover, top barns demand that horses be handled properly and that basic safety rules be followed at all times. You can learn a great deal about how to handle a horse by being with a good barn where high standards are maintained. If you are new to riding, these standards may seem nit-picky at first. They are not—they are there to ensure the safety and well-being of all horses, riders, and visitors. You will soon learn why things must be done (or not done) a certain way. Later on, if you choose to keep your horse at home, you will know how to handle it in a safe and effective manner.

Different stables offer different services, and the cost of riding with a particular establishment often corresponds to the services available. If you are interested in trail riding, look for a barn with access to good trails, and ask if you'll have the chance to ride out with more experienced horsemen. If the answer to both questions is yes, you know you're at least on the right track. If you are interested in riding in horse shows, look for a barn that either puts on its own horse shows or travels to shows on a fairly regular basis. That way you'll be with a barn that can give you the show experience you need.

Once you have found a stable that offers the type of riding you enjoy, the next step is to look around the stable and evaluate it for general safety and cleanliness. Will your horse have the type of accommodations you want it to have? Will the horse be fed at approximately the same time each day? Regular feeding is important to your horse's health, so be sure to ask about the feeding schedule. Will your horse have constant access to fresh water? Will there be a secure place for you to keep your tack and equipment? If you regularly visit the barn after dark, you'll want to ask about lighting. Are the rings lighted for night riding? What about lights in the barns, grooming area, and parking lot? All of these are points to consider.

No stable in the world can accommodate every rider's wishes. The secret to finding the right stable for you is to know where you are willing to be flexible and where you should not compromise. For example, if you know that you'll be riding in the evenings after dark, security and lighting are vital—these are not points on which you can compromise. If trail riding is your primary reason for having a horse, you probably wouldn't be happy in an urban stable with no access to the out-of-doors. By knowing your own goals and objectives before you go stable shopping, you'll be able to make better decisions about which facility is right for you.

Horses and Instructors

If you do not yet own a horse, you'll need to find a riding school that has teaching or "lesson" horses for you to ride. Don't underestimate the importance of a good lesson horse—you'll be amazed at all it has to teach you. No top rider in the world ever started out on an Olympic-level horse. That person first had to learn the basics on an experienced lesson horse. Moreover, most top competitors credit their success not just to their instructors, but also to their lesson horses.

When you visit a stable, ask to see the lesson horses. Are they healthy, clean, and well maintained? Look carefully at the hooves. Are they neatly trimmed? Do the shoes appear to fit? Chances are, the answers to these questions will be yes. Top stables know the value of their lesson horses, and they take good care of their stock. If you're lucky enough to arrive while a lesson is in progress, sit quietly and watch for a few minutes. Do the riders appear to be having a good time as well as learning? If the answer to this question is also yes, you're in the right place.

Photo: Dawn Johnson for USPC

A young girl receives valuable riding tips from her instructor.

Riding instructors, like academic ones, have special areas of interest, so you may find it helpful to ride with an instructor who shares your goals and objectives. Realize, however, that regardless of any special interest, good riding is always based on sound fundamentals. If possible, watch the instructor teach a few lessons. Do the riders wear safety hats and boots or other appropriate footwear? Are the instructor's directions clear and easy to understand? (You may not understand some of the terminology if you're watching an advanced class, but if the *students* understand, they have learned the terms along the way. So will you.) Finally, what are the costs per lesson, and how many times per week are you expected to ride? If these factors fit into your schedule and budget, sign up for lessons as soon as you can. You'll be glad you did.

Centers for Riders with Disabilities

Horseback riding and other equine activities provide challenges as well as rewards for all riders. For riders with disabilities, the challenges are even greater. The North American Riding for the Handicapped Association (NARHA) was formed specifically to help people with disabilities successfully meet these challenges. Founded in 1969 and headquartered in Denver, Colorado, NARHA is dedicated to serving individuals of all ages who have mental, physical, or emotional disabilities. NARHA has more than 450 operating centers throughout the United States and Canada, ranging from small, one-person programs to large operations with a full staff of instructors and therapists.

Therapeutic riding is recognized and embraced by the American Occupational Therapy Association and the American Physical Therapy Association. The benefits of therapeutic riding are available to individuals with almost any disability, and research shows that students who participate in therapeutic riding receive physical, emotional, and mental rewards.

Photo: NARHA

NARHA provides people of different ages and abilities with the chance to develop a relationship with a horse and reap the benefits.

For individuals with impaired mobility, horseback riding gently and rhythmically moves their bodies in a manner similar to walking, thereby improving their balance, muscle control, and overall strength.

In addition to therapeutic riding, many NARHA operating centers offer additional equine activities for those with disabilities, including carriage driving, vaulting, trail riding, equestrian competitions, and/or a study in stable management.

Individuals with learning or mental disabilities are motivated by riding to increase concentration, patience, and discipline. If a psychological or emotional disability is present, the unique relationship formed with a horse can help improve interpersonal relationships, and everyone benefits from improved self-esteem and coping skills. NARHA sets and maintains high safety standards, provides continuing education, and offers networking opportunities for individual and operating-center members.

Horses and ponies participating in NARHA programs are safe, well schooled, and suitable for the task at hand. Riders with disabilities do not need to supply their own horses; NARHA provides each rider with a horse compatible with his/her size and ability.

Operating centers need volunteers, riders, instructors, therapists, horses, and equipment. For information on enrolling an individual in the therapeutic riding program, donating a horse or equipment, or becoming a financial donor or riding-center volunteer, contact NARHA.

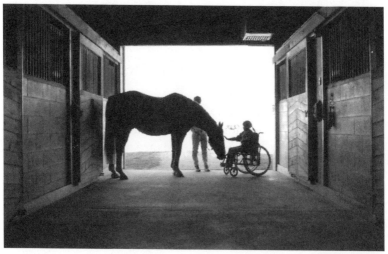

Photo: NARHA

NARHA horses are well suited for participants with disabilities.

Youth Groups

One of the best ways for young enthusiasts to learn about riding and horse care is to join a youth group involved with equestrian activities. One such group is the United States Pony Club (USPC). The USPC uses the term "pony" to reflect its youthful membership, not the size of the animal. Horses and ponies of many different breeds and sizes are seen in Pony Club activities; in some clubs, a member does not have to own a horse or pony to belong.

Photo: Susan Showalter for USPC

The name "Pony Club" reflects the organization's youthful membership, not the size of the animals that are ridden.

Prior knowledge of horses is not required for Pony Club membership. One or more qualified instructors are a part of every Pony Club, and members learn riding skills, stable management, basic veterinary care, and, eventually, competition riding. There are also non-riding activities in which clubs compete, such as quiz-bowl competitions, which test members' knowledge about horses and horse care. The emphasis is on fun as well as on education.

The United States Pony Club is the leading junior equestrian organization in the world, and is represented in 30 countries. In the United States there are more than 600 CCI **** individual clubs throughout the country with more than 12,000 members. Membership is open to any individual up to the age of 21, and volunteers of any age are always welcome. The primary objectives of the Pony Club are to provide instruction in riding and horsemanship, with an emphasis on safety procedures, and to instill in members the ideal of good sportsmanship and the knowledge that will enable them to properly care for and enjoy horses all their lives. For more information contact the USPC.

AHSA Junior and Young Rider Programs

The American Horse Show Association (AHSA) offers many official national championships that encourage up-and-coming riders to reach for the highest levels of competition and achievement. Many Olympic team riders have competed in these championships during their careers, winning these coveted titles. Aspiring show-jumping riders, using the unique American equitation program that is considered a key to U.S. success, aim toward qualifying for and competing in the AHSA/Eisers & Pessoa National Hunter Seat Equitation Medal Championship, the Rolex/Maclay Finals, and, for some, the Rolex/USET Talent Search, held on both coasts. Riders also try for a spot on the four-member teams that are bound each fall for the AHSA's National Junior Jumper Championships, where team experience shapes riders for top international competition. Aspiring three-day eventing riders head for the AHSA's National Junior/Young Rider Championship—East and West, competitors riding against the best in a championship competition and for a chance to reach the top of their age bracket. Young riders in dressage, show jumping, and three-day eventing all compete for a chance to ride at the multinational North American Young Riders' Championship, held each August for talented youngsters in the three Olympic disciplines. More than just a team experience, riders also get a rigorous course in international rules and requirements.

Scholastic Riding Programs

Throughout the nation, high schools, colleges, and universities are forming riding programs and interscholastic equestrian teams. Perhaps one of the best-known programs is the Intercollegiate Horse Show Association (IHSA) and its National Championships, sponsored by Miller's.

Established in 1967 by Robert E. Cacchione, then a student at Fairleigh Dickinson University, the IHSA is founded on the principle that any college student should be able to participate in horse shows regardless of his or her financial status or riding experience. The IHSA promotes competition for riders of all skill levels who compete individually and as teams at regional and national events.

Photo: Miller's

College riders compete for the Intercollegiate Horse Show Association's championship trophy, sponsored by Miller's.

The competition is unique in that all riders are mounted on horses supplied by the host college, with each horse being assigned by lot. Some top performers who have shown for their college teams include Greg Best, University of Pennsylvania; Beezie Patton, Southern Virginia College for Women; and Peter Wylde, Tufts University.

For more information on scholastic riding programs, contact the athletic department of the high school, college, or university of your choice. If they don't already have a riding program, perhaps you could be the person to start one.

4

A Horse of Your Own

Are you already anticipating the day you will get your first horse? If so, you are not alone. Horseback riding is one of the most popular and fastest-growing sports in America. In fact, it may surprise you to learn that more commercial stables are opening up in urban areas than in rural areas, and that's especially good news for city-dwelling horse lovers. After all, one of the big advantages of a commercial stable is that you can get the supervised help you'll need to get started right.

Of course, if you live in a rural area and plan to keep your horse at home, you already have something city dwellers can only imagine: access to open space. Perhaps your dream is to canter your new horse across a green meadow, explore a path through the woods, walk beside a mountain stream, or take a brisk, early morning trot when desert wildflowers are in full bloom. No matter where you live, trail riding allows you to develop a special communication with your horse that no amount of ring work can ever surpass. If you are fortunate enough to be able to take lessons from a qualified instructor *and* have access to a few trails, you really will have the best of both worlds.

If you haven't already purchased an animal, the following may be helpful to you in making your selection.

Goals and Objectives

Probably the single most important issue is to decide what it is you want to accomplish with your new horse. What are your goals and objectives? This may seem obvious, but the issue is complex and deserves a thorough examination. There are many forms of riding and many things that can be accomplished, but to be successful in your endeavor you must first have a horse that is suitable to your purpose. This does *not* mean the most expensive nor the biggest nor even the prettiest horse—it does, however, mean finding the horse best suited to your needs.

Remember that horses, like people, are different from one another, not only in size, shape, and hair color, but in temperament, too. Horses have better hearing and eyesight than people, but they startle easily and don't like loud noises. They are color-blind and farsighted, like some people, so they need time to get used to new objects that are near them. Horses have good memories and learn easily, but the rider must let the horse know what is expected by using hands, legs, weight, and voice to communicate. The secret to success is to find a horse that has the experience, athletic ability, and personality to meet your goals and objectives.

Trail Riding

If your goal is to meander along the trail, savoring the beauties of nature (and that can be a rewarding goal in and of itself), then you need a horse that enjoys being away from the barn; doesn't shy or spook easily; will stand quietly while you mount and dismount; is willing to cross streams, climb rocks, or go up and down hills; and, most important, is not afraid of traffic. If this is your first horse, it's best to purchase one that has experience with all of these situations and has proven to be a quiet, competent trail horse.

It's important for a horse and rider to be well suited for each other.

It's not fun to ride a horse so nervous that it jigs every step of the way, nor so "barn sour" that it won't take a step without constant and vigorous encouragement from the rider. You want a horse you can have fun with. Leave the difficult horses to the more experienced riders—after all, your goal is to have safe, enjoyable trail rides, not pitched battles. A seasoned, well-behaved horse will prove to be a trustworthy companion and a wonderful teacher.

Pleasure Horses

Although some breeds seem to be especially popular for trail riding, almost any breed can be used for this purpose. The individual animal is what is important here, not the breed. Look for experience, athletic ability, and temperament, and don't let yourself get sidetracked with fancy breeding records.

When selecting a trail horse, it is advisable to consider the horse's size relative to your size. If you select an animal so tall that you can't mount without assistance, you're going to be up a creek

Photo: Gary R. Coppage for USPC

A horse and rider enjoy time together away from the stable.

without a paddle if you ever have to dismount to open and close a gate or move an object blocking the trail. You don't want to have to walk all the way home because you couldn't get back on.

One of the most popular breeds for both trail riding and horse shows is the American quarter horse. Its conformation, way of moving, and quiet temperament make the quarter horse an excellent choice for riders of all ages and levels of experience.

Performance Horses

If your goal is to compete in horse shows, combined training events, gymkhanas, or other equestrian competitions, you will need to be more concerned about the breed of horse that you select. Specific types of performance require specific types of athletic ability, and certain breeds are naturally better at some things than they are at others.

Depending on your goals and objectives, you may even have to consider switching from one breed or type of horse to another.

For example, if you've been riding a long-legged Thoroughbred but decide you want to show in western pleasure classes, you're going to have to select another horse—one suitable to the slow, short-striding type of movement desired in the western performance horse. Conversely, if you've been riding a small, short-striding horse but now you want to ride jumpers, you'll need a horse with the athletic ability to leap the obstacles *and* easily cover the distance between fences. A short-legged horse will have a harder time turning in a clean performance and a fast time on a jumper course than will a taller, longer-striding animal.

Some breed associations have their own horse shows. At a breed-specific show, you would need to ride a horse of that particular breed. At non-breed-specific shows, you may ride a horse of any breed, but you would still want to select a horse well suited to that particular activity.

Photo: V. J. Zabek for USCTA

In order to be competitive, an equestrian rider must select a breed of horse that's well suited for the particular competition.

If you're not sure yet what type of riding most appeals to you, spend some time going to a variety of equestrian events. Take in a dressage show and watch the riders and horses "dance as one" in the beautiful musical kur. Visit an Arabian show and watch the native costume class where riders dressed in elaborate Arabian regalia enter the arena at a full gallop—a truly spectacular sight. Go to a western show and observe the quiet, rhythmic action of the pleasure and trail horses, and compare that to the hair-raising spins and slides of the stock horses. For pure heart-stopping action, however, nothing beats Grand Prix jumping. Attending a Grand Prix gives you a good opportunity to see and compare Warmbloods and Thoroughbreds, and to notice how the different breeds are ridden. Generally, the Warmbloods take a little more leg and "push," while the Thoroughbreds are usually ridden with great finesse and a "light seat."

Photo: Jackson Shirley for USDF

European Warmbloods like this Hanoverian gelding make elegant dressage horses.

Since every experience around horses will help you increase your knowledge, try to attend as many different horse shows as you can. Some breed-specific shows, such as Arabian and Morgan, have classes for all three major divisions: hunt seat, stock seat (or western), and saddle seat. Remember, for breed-specific shows and activities, you will need a horse of that particular breed. At open, or non-breed-specific shows, you will see a variety of breeds being ridden, but all will be horses well suited to that particular type of work.

Whenever you are watching equestrian events, pay close attention to the horses themselves and ask yourself two questions: Do these look like horses I would want to ride? Is this style of riding something I would want to do? Answering these questions can help you focus and define your riding goals and objectives.

It will take hours of practice to ride well enough to actually enter a competition, but visiting horse shows is an excellent way to learn about different breeds and different styles of riding. Last but not least, watching the great horses and riders gives you incentive to work hard in your riding lessons. Remember, no one ever woke up one morning suddenly knowing how to ride. The champions got to be champions because they worked at it.

5

Stable Management

Half the fun of owning a horse is taking care of him. Before you buy or lease a horse, decide where your horse will live and how often you can get there to take care of him. If possible, try to stable your horse close to home so that you can check on him every day. Your horse depends on you to provide him with a clean, safe environment; to give him the food, water, and nutritional supplements that his body needs; to provide prompt veterinary aid in the event of an emergency; and to keep his hooves clean, trimmed, and shoed on a regular basis. If your circumstances are such that you can only visit your horse on weekends, you will have to arrange for someone to watch him during the week—domesticated horses simply cannot be left on their own. The reason is that if your horse should become ill or injured, or even tangled in the fence, you wouldn't know it until the weekend, and your horse can't wait that long for help. So, let's say that you have found three or four stables within your area from which to choose. Let's take a closer look at the things you'll want to consider.

Facilities

The four most important considerations are: 1) the type of stabling your horse will have; 2) your access to riding arenas and trails; 3) the presence of on-site trainers, grooms, and other able assistants; and 4) the availability of extras such as a hot walker, cross-ties, tack and feed storage compartments, bath racks, turn-out areas, and lights.

Stabling

There are three types of stabling: 1) indoor stalls; 2) covered paddocks; and 3) open pasture. Of course there are variations on these basics, but those are the most common types of stabling available. Stables don't need to be elaborate, but for overall health, your horse needs openness and a feeling that he is not confined in a space that is too small for him.

Indoor Stalls—This refers to a box stall in a barn. The horse remains enclosed and under cover until someone takes him out— he cannot get out of the box stall by himself. Box stalls range in size from 8 by 10 feet to 14 by 16 feet, with 12 by 12 feet being one of the most common. What is important here is that you get a stall large enough for your particular animal. A Connemara pony, for example, will fit nicely into an 8-by-10-foot stall, but you certainly couldn't stuff a Thoroughbred or a Hanoverian into one that size. If the barn has stalls of more than one size, make sure you tell the stable manager what breed of horse or pony you have, and make sure you will be assigned a stall that meets your needs.

The points you should consider are how often and at what time of day you can visit your horse. If you can come by every day during the daylight hours, an interior stall will make no difference to your horse. But if you can only visit two or three times a week, and even then only in the evening, your horse will never see the sun. Such an arrangement is not healthy for a horse, and you would need a stable where your horse can be taken out during the day.

Construction of the stall is also important. Both the door and the stall must be free of nails, sharp edges, or other snags; the door, regardless of style, should open and close smoothly and securely. If the stall contains a "hayrick" or feed bin, check it for rough edges. If you find any, ask that they be sanded or filed. Most barns today have automatic watering devices. Make sure the water float is working properly and that the bowl is free from leaks.

Covered Paddocks—Covered paddocks are popular at boarding and training stables, and they make a secure shelter for horses kept at home. A covered paddock is an economical alternative to building a full-scale barn. If you are considering building a covered paddock or boarding your horse at a stable where paddocks are available, the following guidelines may be helpful.

If you are looking at space at a boarding stable, be sure the paddock has a good roof that covers at least one-third of the total area. A paddock without a roof is not suitable for permanent stabling. Your horse needs a place to get out of the sun and away from flies and other insects. Horses are capable of withstanding cold weather with no ill effect, but the hot summer sun dries the skin, fades the coat, and saps a horse's energy. If possible, visit the stable during both the morning and afternoon. Check the angle of the sun and be sure that the roof's shadow falls *into* the paddock where your horse can take advantage of it—a shadow cast outside the paddock is of no benefit. Equally important are a clean and continuous supply of drinking water, good footing, adequate drainage, and a securely latching gate.

Open Pasture—Regardless of size, the field must be safe for horses and ponies. The surrounding fence should be at least 4 feet high, strong enough to prevent escape, and made from a material that will not injure any animal that runs into it or leans against it. Barbed wire must never be used around horses. If the fence is sagging, weak, or in any way needs repair, renovations must be completed before animals can be turned out.

Check your pasture at least once a week for debris, and remove any foreign matter whenever you see it. Take a little wagon or a burlap sack around with you and load up—no matter how carefully you clean your pasture, horses' hooves turn up rocks and other objects that may have been buried for years. For safety reasons, any deep holes should be filled before using the pasture, and low spots should be filled and graded as necessary. Low spots gather water, and such water holes are a haven for mosquitoes and other harmful pests.

Salt licks should be available to pastured horses, and there should be more than one source of clean, readily available drinking water. That way, if one source fails, another will be operable while the first is being repaired. Horses and ponies must never be left without drinking water. They can and will become dehydrated very quickly if deprived of water.

Footing and Bedding

Footing refers to the ground in your riding arenas and exercise areas. As with your pasture, any holes or low places should be filled and graded. All rocks and other debris must be removed, and the entire surface should be "combed" on a regular basis.

Whatever form of bedding you use in your stalls and covered paddocks, it should provide insulation, draw moisture, cushion the horse's feet (thereby reducing stress on his legs), and give him a soft bed on which he can lie down and rest. When the horse is lying down, his nose is close to the bedding; therefore, bedding cannot be made of any substance which is overly dusty or which would disturb his breathing. Finally, bedding must be easy to clean. A foul, unkempt stable is disgusting, especially so to the horses. Choose a bedding material that you can toss, clean, and carry away.

Straw is a good insulator and is especially popular as a bedding source in very cold climates. Straw has one drawback, however, in that horses tend to eat it. Since straw is not easy to digest, this may not be a good choice for some horses.

Another popular bedding material is wood shavings. They are warm, clean, gentle on the legs, and economical to buy, either in bales or in bulk. If you buy in bulk, be sure to have an enclosed area for storage, otherwise the first big wind will blow them away. If you choose this source of bedding, make sure to use shavings, not sawdust. Sawdust is so fine that it can cause respiratory problems, and horses don't stay clean when sleeping on it.

Feed and Water

A horse eats about two pounds per day of air-dried feed for every 100 pounds of weight, and the staple of the diet is hay. There are two types of hay: grasses and legumes. Grass hays produce their seeds in "seed heads"; legumes produce theirs in "flowers." Some well-known grass hays are timothy, red clover, Kentucky bluegrass, and orchard grass. Perhaps the best-known legume hay, which is rich in proteins, vitamins, and minerals, is alfalfa. Different types of hay are available in different parts of the country. Grass hays are readily available in the Midwest, but alfalfa is more prevalent in the Southwest. Another feed option is pelleted grain or pelleted hay and grain combined. Pellets might be the feed solution when storage space is a concern. There is also less waste and dust.

Buying Hay

When buying hay, look for clarity in color. Hay should be green and look healthy, without a trace of gray film on the stems or leaves. A gray color indicates mold, and horses must never be allowed to eat any hay (or grain) containing mold; this can cause a life-threatening illness for your horse. Feel the stems and leaves; they should not feel damp or soggy, nor should they feel overly dry. Good hay bends without breaking, gently returning to its upright shape. If the stems snap like dry twigs, they probably are.

The most important test hay must pass is the "smell test"— good hay smells sweet; moldy hay emits an acrid, unpleasant order. Pull a flake apart and smell it, paying particular attention to the center. If it smells bad, don't buy it—not at any price. A nasty odor is a telltale sign of mold.

Letting a horse feed on grass clippings is *not* the same as letting a horse graze on pasture grass. Grass molds and ferments very soon after cutting, and clippings have been known to cause serious illness. No matter how tasty they might look, grass clippings should never be fed to a horse or pony.

Storage

To keep it fresh, hay must be stored up off the ground or floor. Wooden pallets work very well, or you can lay 2-by-6s on the ground and stack the hay on top of them. Do not pack the bales tightly against each other. Arrange them in a cross pattern to encourage air circulation, and always keep hay protected from rain, fog, or dampness. If hay is stored outdoors, a tarp over the hayrick provides good protection. If hay is kept indoors, the building or shed should have good ventilation. Keep bales from touching the walls, so the hay doesn't soak up moisture.

Feeding Schedule

Horses do best when given constant access to hay or pasture grass and allowed to pick and nibble at liberty. This is how horses eat in the wild—wandering along, grazing throughout the day. Unfortunately, it is not always possible to feed domesticated horses this way. Keep your feeding schedule as constant as you possibly can. Your horse should always have at least one hour to digest the food before exercise; two hours is even better. Check the drinking water supply and clean and fill any buckets.

If you supplement your horse's diet with grain, make sure the animal is completely cool, relaxed, and has had a chance to drink water before feeding on grain. For the average horse as described above, six pounds of rolled oats, three pounds of rolled corn, and a general vitamin/mineral supplement make a nice post-workout meal. You can get fancy and top it off with sliced carrots and apples, and your horse will think you are a regular Julia Child. But no matter how much your horse seems to enjoy it, grain is a supplement to, not a replacement for, hay, pasture grass, or other fiber. Feed good quality hay at regular, established feeding times, and you will have a healthy and happy partner.

Grain—For novice horse owners, a ready-mixed feed is probably the safest way to add grain to your horse's diet. There are many excellent brands on the market nationwide. Tell the feed store clerk what breed of horse you have, its age, what type of work it's doing, and how often, and the clerk should be able to direct you to the appropriate grain. For example, the nutritional needs of a Grand Prix jumper will be different from those of a pleasure horse. Also mention if your horse is kept in a box stall or paddock, or if it is kept at pasture where it has plenty of room to roam. These questions are important, because how your horse lives determines the quantity and type of food it should get. Follow the feeding directions on the label and feed at the same time every day.

Grain should be kept in a sealable container, away from excessive heat, dampness, and direct sunlight. If grain starts to mold, it will emit a sour odor. Get rid of it—all of it. You must not feed from a bin where grain has started to mold. Grain bins should be stored on wooden blocks to allow for air circulation under and around the container.

If your normal routine changes for any reason—for example, you stop riding for a month or you move your horse from pasture to barn or vice versa—your horse's diet will have to be modified accordingly. Changes in feed should never be made abruptly, however. A horse needs time to adjust when switching from one diet to another. Consult with your veterinarian, then follow the vet's directions carefully.

Water—As we have discussed, your horse or pony needs to have fresh water available at all times. If you use a tub or bucket, make sure it is cleaned and filled several times a day, especially in hot weather. Rubber and strong plastic are good materials to use around horses, as there are no sharp edges. If you prefer to use a galvanized tub, check it carefully for snags, and line the rim with an old rubber hose. Buckets and tubs should be secured to the stall, paddock, or pasture fence to prevent their being turned over. Bucket holders can be purchased at a tack supply store, but strong elastic cords work just as well. Cords should be snug enough to prevent the horse from getting tangled in them, and secured to the wall or post with eyebolts, not open-end hooks. Eyebolts can be purchased at any hardware or tack supply store.

For horses and ponies at pasture, two or more watering devices are best. Some horses are shy and afraid to approach the "crowd" around the main tank. An alternative water supply allows timid horses a quiet place to drink.

Another option is to install an automatic watering device that enables the horse to fill the bowl when thirsty. The horse does this by pushing on a lever, allowing fresh water to flow into the bowl; a float keeps it from overflowing. Horses learn very quickly how to operate an automatic watering device.

If you live in an area that gets cold enough to freeze, be sure to break the ice off the horse's drinking water each morning. Many horses will not do this for themselves, thereby failing to get the water their bodies need.

6

Care of the Horse

Whether you buy a horse of your own or ride a lesson horse at a riding school, you'll want to know how to give the horse the proper care.

Looking after a horse is a big responsibility, but your job will seem easier if you develop a regular routine for daily care. The benefits of a regular routine are threefold.

- *First*, realize that horses respond very well when they know what to expect from you. As a result of your developing and following a daily routine, your horse will get to know you and trust you, and become easier to handle.

- *Second*, you will get to know him. If any irregularities arise, e.g., the horse develops a sore leg, goes off his feed, or seems out of sorts, you'll notice it right away and be prepared to take the appropriate action.

- *Third*, it's difficult for you to cover all the basics of horse care if you don't know your tools or don't know how to use them. By establishing a routine, you will get so comfortable with your duties that they will become automatic. You won't spend half an hour wandering around, wondering what to do next. Knowing your business saves time, energy, and even money. Let's take a closer look at grooming and the tools you'll need.

Grooming Tools

The main purpose of grooming is to keep the horse clean, but it also tones muscle, stimulates circulation, and contributes to the horse's overall health and fitness. Grooming, then, is an essential part of horse care, and anyone who cannot fit grooming time into his or her schedule would do well to delay buying a horse until such time is available. In the meanwhile, keep on with your lessons and observe the work done by the grooms at your riding school. You can learn a great deal by watching and asking questions.

If you have decided to buy a horse, you will need grooming tools, and that calls for a trip to the tack shop. It is easy to be overwhelmed by the variety of items available, but you can do a highly effective job with just a few essentials.

- *Halter/Lead Rope*—A secure, well-fitting halter is your most important piece of equipment. Halters and lead ropes come in leather, cotton, and nylon. Lead ropes should have a secure snap and be at least 8 feet long.

- *Hoof Pick*—This is used to remove mud, stones, and any other debris from the horse's feet. Always work from the heel toward the toe, and take care not to gouge the center of the foot. This area, known as the *frog*, aids circulation through the foot and leg. To pick up a leg, stand close to the horse, facing the tail. Lean your weight on the horse's shoulder (or hip) as you run your hand along the back of his leg, working downward along the tendons toward the hoof. When he raises his foot, support it with one hand while the other wields the hoof pick. Put the horse's foot down gently when you are finished cleaning, and make sure your own feet are out of the way.

- *Dandy Brush*—This is a stiff brush used primarily for the removal of mud. A dandy brush works well on pastured horses or ponies who have thick coats, but is too coarse for regular use on sleek, thin-skinned horses. If your horse is kept indoors rather than at pasture, you may need it only to brush mud off the hooves. Hold the brush firmly and use short, vigorous, outward strokes, as if whisking lint off a jacket. This brush is too coarse to be used on the face, around the ears, or inside the hind legs.

- *Body Brush*—Softer than the dandy brush, the body brush is the backbone of all grooming aids. You will use this brush every day to remove dirt and dust from all parts of the body. Put some elbow grease into your work and you'll be surprised at how quickly your horse's coat will shine. Short strokes work better than long passes; brush in the direction of the hair. Because you use the body brush every day, it is advisable to replace it about every six months. The other tools need not be replaced as often.

- *Face Brush*—This is a small, very soft brush especially for use around the face and ears. On sensitive horses with very fine coats, it works well as an overall body brush. Because this brush is used around the face, replace it when it shows signs of wear. Worn bristles can break off and get into the horse's eyes and ears. A new brush is far less expensive than a vet bill.

- *Curry Comb*—A plastic or rubber curry comb, used in a vigorous, circular motion, helps remove loose hair. Take care to use it only on well-muscled parts of the body, such as the shoulders, forearms, and hindquarters. Do not use it on the face, along the spine, or on the legs below the knees and hocks. Use the curry comb directly on the horse *only during shedding season*. Otherwise, use it daily to clean body and face brushes. Clean bristles by drawing each brush across the face of the curry comb. Do this several times during each grooming session. Metal curry combs are also available, but they are too severe to use on a horse or pony. Use them only for cleaning brushes. A rubber or plastic curry comb is a better choice for a novice.

- *Sponges*—You will need at least two sponges: a small, soft one to clean the muzzle and around the nostrils; and a larger one for giving your horse a bath. If you have never given a horse a bath, ask an experienced horseman or groom to help you. Some horses are afraid of water and can be difficult to handle. Bathe a horse only where you can secure him in cross-ties and where a butt-bar can be attached to prevent him from pulling back. Never turn a cold hose on a horse's body. Apply water first on the legs, then the hindquarters, then the chest, neck, and finally the body cavity. Wash and rinse the face with the sponge—do not squirt a horse or pony in the face with a hose. Not only is it frightening to him, but a blast of water can damage a horse's eyes and ears.

- *Sweat Scraper*—After bathing and rinsing, use an aluminum or rubber scraper to remove excess water from the coat. Starting at the neck, behind the ears, pull the scraper along the coat, working toward the shoulder. Always work in the direction of the hair. Scrape the body cavity, belly, and hindquarters. Avoid the spine and withers, and do not use it on the legs below the knees and hocks. Dry the face gently with a soft towel. Groom the tail during bathing by first wetting the hair, then applying conditioner. Separate the hairs carefully with your fingers. Rinse and let dry. Brush gently to avoid breakage.

- *Stable Rubber*—This refers to any type of cloth or towel used to give the coat a final polish. Always work in the direction of the hair. You can buy these items under various brands and manufacturers' labels, but an old terry cloth towel from home works just as well. Launder on a regular basis and replace as necessary.

- *Utility Bucket*—Use the utility bucket to store your grooming tools. Plastic or lightweight rubber is safer to use around horses than galvanized steel, and doesn't make as much noise when items are dropped in. Some tack shops sell wooden or plastic boxes to hold grooming tools, but a bucket is usually cheaper and easier to carry, and serves double duty if you should need to haul water. When it's time for a bath, mix your shampoo and water in the utility bucket, and use your large sponge to wash your horse. After you are finished, rinse the bucket thoroughly before putting it away. You will find many practical uses for a good utility bucket. But do not use your utility bucket as a feed bucket. Get separate buckets for your horse's feed and drinking water, and do not use them for anything else.

Photo: Betty Skipper for USPC

Grooming is an essential part of all-around horsemanship.
Use a curry comb made of rubber or plastic rather than metal.

Other grooming items you may want to have handy are: a leather punch; a scissors for opening feed bags (keep it away from your horse); a flashlight; a mitt or towel for applying fly repellent or liniment; and an aluminum mane comb for grooming the mane, forelock, and tail (be careful not to pull hairs out of the tail).

Veterinary and Stable Supplies

While you're in the tack shop buying your grooming tools, take that opportunity to pick up the basic veterinary and stable supplies every horse owner should have on hand. As with grooming tools, don't be overwhelmed by the variety of items available. The following basics will get you off to a good start.

- *Fly Repellent*—Many good brands are available, but even the best won't help your horse if you don't apply it on a regular basis. Fly repellent can be sprayed on or rubbed on using a mitt or towel. Most spray-on types need to be diluted with water. You can buy a plastic container with a pump-type spray attachment. Mix your fly repellent right in the container, then spray it on. Be careful not to get it in your horse's eyes or nose. Spray the mixture onto a mitt or towel, then gently wipe his face and ears.

- *Hoof Dressing*—If your horse tends toward dry, brittle hooves, you'll want a dressing that puts moisture back into the hoof. If your horse tends toward moist, mushy hooves, you'll want a dressing that acts as a drying agent. As a rule of thumb, if your horse lives and works on dry, sandy soil, use a lanolin-based moisture dressing. If your horse lives and works in damp, soggy soil, use a pine-tar-based dressing. If you're not sure of the condition of your horse's hooves, don't buy anything until you've talked with your blacksmith and/or veterinarian. Follow their suggestions.

- *Thrush Dressing*—Thrush is a fungus that can develop in a wet or dirty hoof. If left untreated, thrush can cause lameness. You will recognize its presence by the foul odor emitting from your horse's hoof. Thrush can be prevented by cleaning the hooves daily and by keeping footing and bedding clean and dry. If thrush develops in spite of your efforts, it can be treated in most cases by applying a thrush dressing. Several good ones are on the market; ask your veterinarian for a recommendation. Read the label and follow the directions for application.

- *Topical Infection/Abrasion Dressing*—If your horse should get a minor scratch, an abrasion dressing can be safely applied. The primary benefit of a topical dressing is that it helps keep flies and dirt out of the wound. For anything other than a minor laceration, call your veterinarian.

- *Shampoo/Conditioner*—Do not use human hair products on horses. Equine shampoo is pH balanced for a horse's skin. Human shampoo is very hard to rinse out of a horse's skin and can even make the horse sick. There are many excellent equine shampoos and coat conditioners on the market. Let your budget be your guide.

- *Liniment*—After a workout your horse will welcome a relaxing rubdown. To make a body wash, add one-half-cup of liniment to one gallon of water. (Use your utility bucket.) Dip your large sponge into the mixture, wring, and apply to the neck, body, and legs. If the weather is cool or windy, cover your horse with a wool cooler and walk him until he's dry. Do not put a horse away when his coat is still very damp. Do not apply liniment if a leg feels unusually warm; liniment will just make it hotter. Ice the leg instead, or run cool water over it for at least twenty minutes. If you don't notice improvement within 24 hours, call your veterinarian.

- *Equine Thermometer*—You can and should learn to take a horse's temperature, but do not try it until you have been shown how by an experienced horseman or your veterinarian. Never use a human thermometer—it is not made for horses. Equine thermometers can be purchased at your tack shop. Knowing how to take a horse's temperature is a valuable lesson to learn. It can help you determine the severity of a horse's illness. When you report your findings to your veterinarian, the vet will use that information to guide you as to what you should do until he arrives.

Other all-purpose supplies you can purchase either at a tack shop or drugstore are: hydrogen peroxide (good for washing superficial wounds); cotton balls; rubbing alcohol (has the opposite effect of liniment—use full strength or diluted as a wash to cool the legs); and petroleum jelly (apply to coat where hair has rubbed off).

Health Maintenance

You can help keep your horse healthy by establishing and following a three-step, semiannual veterinary maintenance program.

- *First*, have your veterinarian treat your horse for worms at least twice a year. The vet will do this by *tubing* the horse with an anti-worm medication. Tubing is not something you can or should do on your own, but ask your veterinarian if you can use a paste or powder wormer in between professional treatments. Follow directions carefully and use only the products your veterinarian recommends.

- *Second*, have your horse's teeth checked. Horses often develop sharp points on their back teeth, making it hard for them to chew their food. These sharp points must be filed down. Filing, also known as *floating* the teeth, is essential for good health. If a horse cannot work saliva into the food before swallowing, the food cannot be properly digested, and this interruption in the digestive cycle can lead to colic. The chances of colic can be lessened by regular worming and floating the teeth. Only your veterinarian is qualified to float the teeth. This is not something you can or should do yourself.

- *Third*, establish a semiannual schedule for your horse to receive vaccinations and/or inoculations. These are usually given by injection. Again, only your veterinarian is qualified to administer this treatment. Sometimes a horse needs to be rested completely or worked only lightly after getting the "shots." Ask what follow-up care your horse will need regarding riding, feeding, and turnout.

Do not neglect any part of this three-step veterinary treatment program. It is essential to your horse's health. Remember the old adage: An ounce of prevention is worth a pound of cure. No doubt your horse would agree.

Drugs and Doping

Horses are subject to drug tests, while the Anti-Doping Code of the Olympic Movement applies to all riders at the Games. In addition, the Fédération Equestre Internationale (FEI) has established a Code of Conduct to ensure the health, safety, and well-being of horses.

- The horse, and its welfare, are primary. Its needs take precedence over the needs of everyone else.
- The highest standards of care are to be promoted and maintained.
- Horses must be transported in a safe and healthy manner.
- Riders must be fit and competent.
- Horses must not be abused; they must be respected.
- Education should be ongoing for everyone involved with the health, safety, and well-being of horses.

Shoeing and Hoof Care

One of the most important elements of good horse management is regular hoof care. Your horse simply cannot perform his best if his feet hurt. Badly shoed, poorly trimmed, or injured hooves left untreated are among the most common causes of lameness.

Every time you groom your horse, examine each foot, top and bottom. Use your hoof pick to clean debris from the sole, being careful not to gouge the frog. Use your dandy brush to remove dried mud from around the top of the hoof, called the *coronet*, and from the bulbs of the heels. Apply hoof dressing as directed by your blacksmith or veterinarian.

The feet should be checked and cleaned before and after each ride, especially after a trail ride. It's always possible to pick up a stone or wood chip along the trail. Check to see that the shoes are not loose or twisted, or that your horse hasn't lost a shoe along the way. If you discover that a shoe is loose, twisted, or missing, call your blacksmith right away; do not ride your horse again until the damage has been repaired. Riding with a damaged or missing shoe could cause serious injury, even lameness.

Your horse should be trimmed and re-shoed about every four to six weeks. The horse's age, the type of work he does, and the ground conditions or *footing* on which you usually ride will affect your shoeing schedule. It does not hurt your horse to be shoed.

The shoes are held on by nails, and the nails are driven into the *wall*, the outermost portion of the hoof.

There are no nerve endings in the wall. Your blacksmith can trim the wall and nail on the shoes without causing your horse or pony any pain. In fact, shoes actually help protect the hooves and are regularly used on riding horses. Some barns do allow brood mares to go barefoot, but if your horse is being ridden or worked, shoes will help protect the hooves.

How Shoes Are Selected

Shoes come in different weights, sizes, and even shapes. Some are flat on the bottom; some are rounded. The height, weight, age, and type of work a horse does, along with the overall shape and development of the legs and hooves, determine what type of shoe the horse should wear. Racehorses, for example, wear very thin shoes made of lightweight aluminum. This type of shoe is called a *racing plate*. Draft horses, by contrast, wear heavy

Photo: Hagerty Photo

It takes years of hard work to become a skilled horseshoer.

iron shoes, often outfitted with toe clips and heel caulks to help hold them on. To improve traction for horses working on wet grass, *studs* can be screwed into the shoes. Studs function much like cleats on a golfer's shoes. Studs come in various lengths and sizes, and can be removed from the shoe entirely when not needed.

Many decisions must be made before the actual work of shoeing begins. First, the blacksmith will watch the horse move and ask what type of work the horse normally does. That information will help him decide how he will trim and shape the hooves. When the hooves have been shortened, the blacksmith will select and fit a shoe. The best work is always done by *hot shoeing*. That means the shoe is placed in a forge and heated, then molded to the hoof. The shoe may pass between the anvil and the forge several times before the blacksmith has it just the way he wants it to fit. It takes time, but hot shoeing ensures the most accurate fit. Another type of shoeing is called *cold shoeing*, in which a ready-made shoe is simply fitted to the foot. Cold shoeing will do in a pinch but is not as accurate as hot shoeing for obvious reasons.

A blacksmith must attend shoeing school to learn his or her craft. It takes a long time and is a real art, and anyone who has ever won a blue ribbon knows that part of the credit must go to the horseshoer. Your blacksmith, like your veterinarian, is an important part of your team. Follow his or her advice about trimming, shoeing, and hoof care.

7

Tack and Horse Clothing

When humans first began to domesticate the horse, they soon found that they needed some means of controlling the animal's movement. Throughout the centuries, many devices (some effective, some absurd) were developed to accomplish that objective. These various and sundry devices for controlling (and eventually riding) the horse have come to be known collectively as *tack*.

In contemporary terms, tack generally refers to the saddle and bridle (headstall and reins) and their immediate auxiliaries, such as girths, pads, leathers and irons, martingales, and bits. In a separate category, leg wraps, blankets, day sheets, boots, and the like are referred to as horse clothing. Items in this latter group have to do with the welfare and upkeep of the horse.

Bridles and Bits

The earliest bridles were little more than ropes woven of hair, twigs, and leaves. These ropes were wrapped around the horse's lower jaw, or around the nose and jaw. Over time, as people learned how to tan, cut, and stitch leather hides, the browband, crownpiece, throatlatch, cavesson, and reins were developed.

On early bridles, these pieces were sewn together, but people eventually learned how to make metal buckles. These were used to join the various pieces, thereby making the bridle adjustable. That application is still in use today. The various components of a headstall can be shortened or lengthened, allowing the bridle to fit more than one horse.

The history and development of bits is a well-researched topic, and most tack shops and libraries carry books on this subject. The following describes five bits and bridles commonly used on riding horses.

Snaffle

The snaffle is perhaps the simplest bit for the rider to operate, since it is activated by a single rein. The primary division within the ranks of the snaffle is between those that are joined in the middle (jointed snaffle) and those that are straight ("mullen mouth" snaffle), the latter being the milder of the two.

Snaffles are made in a variety of weights, ranging from the thin *bridoon* (used with a double bridle) to the thick hollow-mouth used for schooling young horses. Snaffle mouthpieces come in an enormous variety of styles: "roller mouth," "slow twist," "corkscrew," the Dr. Bristol, and the "twisted wire." They are made from a variety of materials: stainless steel, copper, soft rubber, and vulcanite (a hard rubber).

Snaffle cheekpieces come in a variety of styles, including full cheek, "D"-ring, "egg butt," and loose ring. (One other snaffle sometimes used on jumpers and horses in the cross-country phase of eventing is the "gag," but this is a very sophisticated bit and should be used by advanced riders only.)

Pelham

The pelham combines the effects of snaffle and curb into one mouthpiece. It may seem a little more awkward for the novice rider in that it uses two reins, the wider attached to the snaffle (or upper) ring on the cheekpiece, the thinner attached to the curb (or lower) ring. The result is that with a pelham, the rider has two reins in each hand, whereas with the snaffle, the rider has but one rein in each hand. When the snaffle rein predominates, the effect is much like that of a snaffle bridle—pressure is applied to the corners of the horse's mouth. When the curb rein predominates, it causes the *shanks* (cheekpieces) to swivel, putting pressure on the *poll* (the top of the horse's head) and brings the curb chain into play under the horse's lower jaw.

Double Bridle

A double bridle is composed of two separate bits: a bridoon and a curb. Both bits fit into the horse's mouth. At first glance, the curb looks similar to a pelham. But on the curb, there is no ring to which you could attach the snaffle rein. The double bridle is used for well-trained dressage horses showing at the third level or above. It is a rather advanced piece of equipment, and a novice rider would do better with a plain snaffle bit or a pelham.

Kimberwick

The Kimberwick gives the leverage effect of a pelham but, like the snaffle, requires only one rein. It has a curb chain, as does the pelham, but the shanks are very short and the leverage is considerably less than that produced by the pelham or curb. The mouthpiece comes in various styles and materials, including jointed mouth, mullen mouth, and roller mouth.

Hackamore

The bitless bridle is perhaps the oldest of all devices. The Spanish hackamore, called the *bosal*, is often made of rope or horsehair, and has a single rein coming from the back of the noseband.

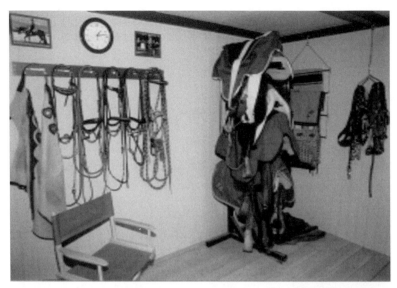

Photo: Hagerty Photo

A clean, tidy tack room reflects good stable management. Note the bosal-type hackamore on the far right of the bridle rack.

The mechanical hackamore is usually made of nylon or leather. The reins are attached to metal shanks, one rein on each side. Contrary to what many people think, a hackamore is not the gentlest or kindest form of bridle. A hackamore operates by putting pressure on the delicate nose cartilage. If used roughly, it can cause a great deal of harm. Unless your horse or pony has been professionally trained with a hackamore, you'll probably be better off with a snaffle bridle, especially in the early stages of your riding.

Saddles

The saddle is a much more recent invention than the bridle, and stirrups are the most recent invention of all. Elaborate versions of the bridle can be traced to the fifth century B.C., but it wasn't until the fourth century A.D. that a saddle was built on a leather-covered wooden frame. One hundred years later the first stirrup was attached. Originally, there was only one stirrup, not because men rode sidesaddle, but because they saw its usefulness only for mounting and dismounting. They quickly discovered, however, that a stirrup helped the rider balance, and if one stirrup was good, two would be even better. The cavalry liked them because stirrups made it more difficult for an enemy to dislodge a soldier from his horse. The new invention took root, and since the fifth century A.D., all cross saddles have been designed to accommodate two stirrups, one on each side. As with bridles and bits, saddles have a long and colorful history.

- *Dressage*—The dressage has the deepest seat of all modern saddles. That means the seat is considerably lower than the pommel (front) and the cantle (rear). The stirrup leathers are inset a little further toward the cantle than they are on other saddles, positioning the rider's legs well back under the hips. A dressage saddle often has very long billets, allowing the girth to buckle by the rider's foot rather than up under the thigh. This overall design gives the rider a very secure feeling and allows excellent communication with the horse.

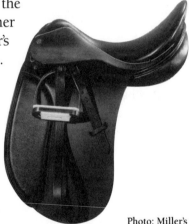

Photo: Miller's

The dressage saddle has a deep seat and long, straight flaps.

- *Close Contact*—The close contact is also known as the forward seat or jumping saddle. The shallower seat and forward cut of the flaps allow the rider to be in balance with the horse when moving at high speed and over fences. When a horse is jumping, its balance shifts considerably farther forward than that of the dressage horse in action; hence the rider needs a saddle that allows him to shift his weight forward in time with his horse. The deep seat and straight flap of the dressage saddle would not allow the rider to move forward enough to be in balance with the movements of a jumper. Likewise, the shallow seat of the forward seat saddle would not position a rider properly for the collected movements of dressage.

Photo: Miller's.

A close contact saddle has a shallow seat and forward-cut flaps.

* *All-Purpose*—This saddle usually comes with adjustable bars, allowing the rider to move the stirrup leather forward or backward, depending on the type of riding. The seat is a cross between the deep pocket of a dressage saddle and the shallow seat of a jumping saddle. The flaps are not as straight as those on a dressage saddle, nor as forward as those on a jumping saddle. The girth, however, usually buckles under the rider's thigh as it does on a jumping saddle.

Photo: Miller's

An all-purpose saddle combines the deep seat of the dressage saddle with the forward-cut flaps of a close contact saddle.

Commonly Used Aids

It is a rare horse that goes all the way through its training wearing only a bridle and saddle. Horsemen everywhere are quick to employ artificial aids to enhance their control and improve their horse's performance. Some of the most commonly used aids are spurs, martingales, breastplates, and nosebands.

- *Spurs*—These are devices, usually of metal, that attach to the heels of a rider's boots. Spurs come in a variety of styles, but the most common is the Prince of Wales. Novice riders should avoid wearing spurs until they have learned to keep their feet and legs quiet and under control.

- *Martingales*—The martingale comes in two styles: standing and running. The standing martingale attaches to the girth and extends forward between the horse's front legs, attaching again at the back of the cavesson. Between the legs and the cavesson, the martingale passes through a thin strap which goes around the horse's neck. This strap holds the martingale close to the underside of the neck, thereby preventing a foreleg from getting tangled in the martingale. It acts to prevent the horse from raising his head so high that he evades the bit. When green horses are first learning to jump, they often lean on the martingale to help them find their balance. Eventually they learn to carry their own balance and no longer require the aid of a standing martingale. Hunters are often shown in a standing martingale.

The running martingale attaches to the girth as described above and also passes forward through the front legs, but it then forks, forming two short straps, each with a ring on the end. The snaffle reins pass through these rings, allowing the martingale to "run" the length

Photo: Miller's

A horse wearing a snaffle bridle fitted with a flash noseband.

of the rein. (Rubber rein stops should be used close to the bit to prevent the martingale rings from catching on the bit.) The effect is to prevent the horse from raising his head, but with a running martingale, the action is on the mouth, not the nose. Jumpers may compete wearing a running martingale.

- *Breastplates*—The breastplate is a device for keeping the saddle in place. To visualize the breastplate, think of the letter "V" with a tail and a short strap connecting the two uppermost points of the V. The horse sticks his head through the V, and the short strap lays across his neck just above the withers. The short neck strap is attached to "D" rings on either side of the saddle. The tail of the V is a strap that passes backward through his front legs and attaches to the girth. Horses competing in jumping and eventing sometimes use a breastplate that wraps around the front of the horse's chest, thereby giving its purchase on the saddle a lower center of gravity.

- *Nosebands*—The noseband comes in a wide variety of configurations. Its primary purpose, regardless of style, is to prevent the horse from opening the mouth far enough to evade the bit. Jumpers often use a figure-eight-style noseband, while dressage riders prefer the "flash" or "dropped" noseband.

Horse Clothing

Horse clothes are those items that enhance the horse's welfare and upkeep, such as blankets, bandages, and boots.

- *Blankets*—The heaviest ones are waterproof and lined with wool. These can be used on horses kept at pasture or with free access to the outdoors. For horses kept indoors, woven or nylon blankets are popular, but non-waterproof materials are not suitable for horses kept outdoors.

- *Sheets*—A lightweight version of the blanket, the "day sheet" provides warmth in cool weather. The "fly sheet" (a lighter weight than the day sheet) prevents insects from biting and can be worn by the horse in warm weather to help keep clean.

- *Coolers*—A cooler is a loose-fitting wool wrap that keeps a hot and/or damp horse from getting a chill. When horses have been bathed, coolers should be put on them while they dry, especially if a breeze is blowing.

- *Bandages*—If ever there was a catchall word, this is it. A bandage is not limited to a dressing applied over a wound, as the name would suggest. Rather, it means any wrap used on the legs or tail. A tail bandage keeps a horse from rubbing the hair off the tail, and can be especially helpful when a horse is being shipped in a van or trailer. Leg bandages can be used for medicinal purposes but are just as frequently used to warm, cool, or support a leg. Ask your veterinarian or an experienced groom to show you how to properly apply a bandage. Never use the type of elastic bandage intended for humans on a horse; they contract too much for equine circulation.

- *Boots*—The primary purpose of boots is to protect the horse's legs from injury. Boots are different from bandages, in that boots are fitted items while bandages are simply long strips of material skillfully wrapped around the horse's legs. Boots have shape and form, and each type of boot is designed to protect a different part of the horse's body. Shipping boots, for example, reach from the hoof to the knee or hock. They are worn whenever the horse is transported in a van or trailer. Bell boots fit over the front hooves and protect the tender heel area from being kicked by the toe of a hind foot. The horse wears these when being ridden or exercised.

Cleaning and Storing

Care of tack and other equipment is an essential part of good stable management. Riding with worn or broken tack is dangerous, and ill-fitting horse clothing can result in sores and injuries. The best approach is to examine all tack before and after each ride. If you notice that stitching is coming loose or that buckles are no longer closing securely, take the item to a saddler and have it repaired before the problem gets any worse. Not only will you save money (extensive repairs get expensive), you'll reduce the chances of having the piece break while you are riding. You can prolong the shine on bits by rinsing and drying them with a soft cloth after every ride.

For proper maintenance of horse tack, you'll need the following items:

- A sponge and utility bucket
- Saddle soap or other leather-cleaning agent
- Leather oil and a small paintbrush
- Mild dishwashing liquid
- A small, stiff brush to remove sweat and hair
- Two clean terry cloth rags (old washcloths are ideal)

Start by disassembling your tack. Remove the pad, stirrup leathers, irons, and girth from the saddle. Disassemble the bridle: headstall, reins, and bit. Remove the spurs from your boots.

Pour warm water into your bucket and add a capful of mild dishwashing liquid. Allow the bit, irons, and spurs to soak a moment, then rub with a clean terry cloth rag. Rinse thoroughly, especially the bit, and, with your second rag, dry immediately. If you wish, you may apply metal polish to your spurs and irons, but if you buy stainless steel, it shines with just a good rubbing. Never put metal polish on the mouthpiece of your bit. Your horse can pick up chemicals from the polish. When you have finished, lay these items aside.

Next, use the small brush to remove any hair, sweat, or grit from the leather, paying careful attention to the underside of the girth. If you use a breastplate or martingale, it should be brushed and cleaned as well.

Empty your bucket and put in a small amount of fresh water. You won't need much, as your objective is only to dampen and rinse your sponge. Wipe the leather with a damp (not soggy) sponge. For general cleaning, apply saddle soap (or a good leather cleaner) to your sponge and wipe again. Don't let the leather get too wet—what you need here is elbow grease, not water. Rub thoroughly and leave all leather pieces in a clean, sheltered place to dry. Do not put your tack out in the sun or next to a heater—the leather will crack. To reduce drying time and protect the leather, wring your sponge well and avoid letting the leather get too wet. When you have finished, let your tack dry for a few hours, overnight if possible. Finally, rub gently with a dry cloth and reassemble.

Make sure all buckles are fastened securely and that the bit is not put on the headstall backward (it's easy to do). Before you ride, check that the bit hangs evenly in the horse's mouth and that your irons hang evenly on your saddle. Readjust cheekpieces and stirrup leathers, if necessary.

Two or three times a year, apply a good leather oil. Use the stiff brush to remove dirt and hair, then wipe all leather parts with a damp sponge. Warm the oil in a double boiler, then brush it on with the paintbrush. Rub it in with your fingers. Let dry at least overnight; two nights are better. Wipe again with a lightly damp sponge, then apply saddle soap as above. Polish with a dry cloth and reassemble.

Blankets, sheets, coolers, saddle pads, and bandages need to be kept clean and free from rips. Wash horse clothing regularly in a mild laundry detergent, and make sure all items are thoroughly dry before storing. Unlike leather, cotton items love the sun and can be safely laid out for airing and drying. Keep all items in good repair.

Tack and horse clothing should be stored in a clean, dry environment with good ventilation. Do not expose tack to excessive heat or moisture, and wash all horse clothing items before packing them away in a trunk or tack box. If you take good care of your equipment, it will serve you well for many, many years.

8

Riding Attire

Perhaps the two most important considerations when selecting riding attire are safety and comfort. By no means is it necessary to wear the latest fashion or the most expensive brand of apparel, but it is worthwhile to invest in a few items. Let's take a closer look at what you'll need to get started.

Protective Wear

For English riding, a well-fitting hard hat with a chin strap is essential. Your skull is fragile, and a hard hat will help protect you in the event of a fall or other accident. No matter how well you ride or how long you've been around horses, always wear your hard hat and fasten the chin strap.

Photo: Miller's.

A safety helmet, known as a "hard hat," is an essential piece of riding attire.

Photos: Miller's

Hunt boots reach the back of the knees.   **Paddock boots extend just above the ankles.**

Next on the list of essentials is proper footwear. This has nothing to do with fashion; riding boots are designed to give your feet, ankles, and legs the support they need for effective communication with the horse and maximum performance. If you're just getting started, you need not buy expensive custom-made boots; boots do influence performance, however, so get the best fit you possibly can. Most tack shops offer a good selection, and you can choose from rubber boots (excellent for wet-weather riding), hunting boots, paddock boots, or heeled riding sneakers. Never ride in flat-soled shoes of any type—your foot could easily slip through the iron.

Gloves are optional, but they do help protect your hands, and many riders feel that gloves improve their grip on the reins. As with boots, most tack shops have a wide selection to choose from, including those made of leather, suede, cotton, knit, and stretch fabrics. For horse shows you'll want leather gloves, but for casual riding, wear whatever feels most comfortable. Riding gloves fit snugly in order to provide the right feel on the reins.

Photos: Miller's

Leather palms with cotton
backs are comfortable in
warm weather.

All-leather gloves are popular
with horse show riders.

For your comfort and safety, remove any rings before putting on your gloves.

If you ride after dark, wear a reflector vest—it makes you more visible to oncoming traffic. Reflector vests are lightweight, fit over your clothing, and do not hinder your riding in any way. Reflector leg wraps are also available for your horse's legs, and these, along with a rider's vest, increase your margin of safety.

For Casual Riding

Whether you are going on a trail ride or working in the ring, you'll want to be comfortable. Riding breeches, whether casual or formal, are cut differently from regular pants; specifically, breeches have no inseam. Their unique cut allows them to lie flat under your thighs and legs, thereby avoiding the irritation of sitting on a seam. Many riders find breeches more comfortable than any other type of trouser. Several clothing manufacturers offer a line of riding breeches that look and feel like soft blue jeans. As these pants are machine washable and very durable, you may find them to your liking.

T-shirts or sports shirts are always popular, and sleeve length is up to you. If the weather is hot, sleeveless tops are perfectly acceptable for casual riding, but you may want to apply a sunscreen on your arms and shoulders to avoid getting burned. Many riders use a sun protection product no matter what the weather.

If the day is cool or windy, you may want to wear a sweater or jacket. If you have to remove clothing while in the middle of the ride, either dismount first or have someone on the ground hold the horse while you remove the clothing. A horse can be spooked while your arms are momentarily immobilized or your face is covered, preventing you from immediately controlling the animal. If you take off a piece of clothing, do not leave it hanging on a fence post or on a jump in the ring—the wind could blow it off, causing the horse to bolt.

It's a good idea to leave fine jewelry at home. You don't want to get a beautiful piece of jewelry full of dust and dirt, and if you should lose it on the trail it may be very difficult to locate. If you normally wear a nice watch, you may want to buy an inexpensive sports watch to wear around the barn. As for safety, avoid wearing necklaces or long earrings that could catch on bridle reins or other pieces of equipment.

Some riders like to wear chaps for schooling and trail riding. Chaps are offered ready-made to the English riding market, but most active competitive riders have custom chaps, often made up in shades of brown, black, green, gray, and blue, with fringe and contrasting color piping and trim. True, the basic colors are not as bright as their Western cousins, but color and decoration abound, and are restrained only by the traditional conservatism of the English riding world. Chaps, as well as tall boots and breeches, provide a textured, snug legging that protects the mounted leg from friction rubs that come from a twisted pant leg and from stirrup leathers that can pinch. They also help the rider's leg to stay properly positioned against the horse instead of sliding about.

There are several styles of raincoats and outerwear on the market today, and no doubt your choice will be influenced as much by the weather in your area as by personal taste. Riding raincoats, like breeches, have a different cut; they are not regular rain garments. They are cut with a "saddle fan" that protects your saddle and keeps the coat from sliding up your legs. Most tack shops offer a good variety.

For Horse Shows

Attire for competition riding could take an entire book by itself. Let's concentrate on what you'll need for your first schooling show.

Under the rules of the American Horse Shows Association, junior riders may not compete without a hard hat with a chin strap in place. Adult riders also are required to wear a hard hat, although the chin strap is optional.

As for your clothing, teenagers and adults will need breeches and knee-high hunt boots for competition riding. Children may wear jodhpur pants and jodhpur boots. Jodhpur pants (riding pants made with extra room in the thighs) should be worn with garter straps and pant clips. Jodhpur boots, like paddock boots, cover the ankle but do not extend up to the knee. Jodhpur boots may be brown or black, but hunt boots most often are black. There are two types of hunt boots: dress boots and field boots. Dress boots are smooth; field boots lace over the instep. Most riders choose dress boots, as these can be worn in all phases of English riding. Field boots are never worn in dressage competitions, but many combined-training riders prefer the adjustment capability of field boots for the cross-country phase of eventing.

For dressage shows, you'll need white breeches. In advanced dressage, your jacket must be black, but at the beginner level your jacket may be navy or charcoal gray. A white "ratcatcher" shirt (the informal shirt worn during fox hunts) is required for both males and females. Men and boys wear either a white stock tie or a regular tie of any dark color; women and girls wear either a white stock tie or a white choker. Your hair should not touch the back of your collar. Pin your hair up and wear a net, if necessary. At the beginner level, gloves are optional. If worn, they should be leather and of a dark color. White gloves, top hats, and tails are worn only for advanced dressage.

For hunter/jumper schooling shows, you'll need breeches and boots as described above; a ratcatcher shirt, which may be pastel or patterned; a dark jacket (also called a hunt coat); and, for females, a stock pin. The pin is worn on the choker in the center of the throat. Male riders wear a regular tie with a tie clasp. Earrings, if worn, must be small and discreet. Necklaces, if worn, should be kept tucked inside your shirt. Bracelets should not be worn. Gloves are optional.

There is much that can be said about proper horse show turnout, or dress, but this will get you started in the right direction. Just be aware that as you advance, turnout will become more critical to your success.

9

First Aid and Safety

Although riding is not considered a contact sport, anyone involved in sports knows that an injury can happen to anyone at any time. Fortunately, most riding-related injuries are not serious, but never take a chance with an injured person. The following guidelines will help everyone deal successfully with an injury around the barn or on the trail:

- *Remain Calm.* The injured rider's recovery may depend on the decisions you make, and it's hard to make accurate decisions when you're flustered. Moreover, your behavior may determine the reactions of others around you, including riders, parents, and spectators. No one will benefit if people are running around, screaming.

- *Stay in Control.* Resist the urge to move an injured rider to a more comfortable location (such as under a shade tree or into the barn). Moving an injured rider could compound the injury. Unless the person is in imminent danger at that particular spot, let the injured rider stay there until help arrives. Whenever there is any doubt as to the nature or extent of an injury, call for emergency assistance (fire, police, and so on).

- *Catch the Horse.* As soon as possible, catch the rider's horse and get it in off the street—for its own safety as well as for the safety of others. If you cannot leave the injured rider, dispatch someone else to catch the horse and lead it, not ride it, back to the barn. The horse is probably too upset at this point to respond well to an inexperienced rider. Let's not have another accident.

The First Aid Kit

It's a good idea to keep a basic first aid kit on hand at all times. Many pharmacies and sporting goods stores carry well-stocked first aid kits that would be fine for barn use. If you want to put one together yourself, the following items should be included:

- Adhesive bandages of various sizes
- Ammonia caps (for dizziness)
- Antiseptic soap (for washing a wounded area)
- Antiseptic solution (for bug bites and minor scrapes)
- Aspirin
- A blanket to cover an injured rider (warmth reduces the chance of shock)
- Cold packs
- Elastic bandages (various sizes)
- Eyewash solution
- Gauze pads (various sizes)
- "Hank's solution" (trade name Save-a-Tooth®)
- Sterile cotton sheets (can be cut to fit)
- Scissors
- Tissues and pre-moistened towelettes
- Tweezers (for splinters)
- Utility knife, *e.g.*, Swiss army knife to take on trail rides

The phone number of the nearest ambulance service should be taped to the inside of your first aid kit. All riders and barn workers should know where the first aid kit is stored, and where it will be kept at horse shows and other events. The best first aid kit in the world does you no good if you can't find it when you need it. Make sure someone knows the location of the closest telephone, and always keep some change in the kit, so you won't have to hunt for coins in an emergency.

Handling a Dislodged Tooth

Most of the time when a tooth has been knocked out, it can be replanted and retained for life, especially if the tooth has been properly handled. One critical factor in achieving a successful replant is the care and handling of a dislodged tooth.

The best way to store a tooth is to immerse it in a pH-balanced buffered cell-preserving solution, such as Hank's or Viaspan® (used for transplant organ storage). Hank's solution (under the trade name Save-a-Tooth®) may be purchased over the counter at many drugstores. With the use of a proper storage and carrying container, there is an excellent chance of having a dislodged tooth successfully replanted.

Vision and Corrective Lenses

Your vision, just like the strength in your arms and legs, is an important part of your overall performance, and the demands on your vision during sporting activities are rigorous. To ride your best, you must know what's behind you, beside you, and in front of you at all times, and this takes a variety of visual skills. If your natural vision inhibits your athletic performance, ask your doctor about corrective lenses.

Today's eye-care practitioners use a wide variety of lens materials. Among them are the new impact-resistant lenses now available for use in prescription glasses. These lenses are cosmetically excellent, reasonable in cost, lightweight, and will not shatter if broken.

Another option is contact lenses. Available in hard and soft lens materials, contacts offer many excellent advantages to the athlete. For best results, tell your doctor about the type (or types) of riding that you do. That information will be helpful to the doctor in selecting the best lenses for you. If you wear contact lenses, take your cleaning and wetting solutions with you to all equestrian events, and notify your riding instructor that you are wearing contacts. Instructors, as well as riders and parents, should have a basic understanding of how to remove, insert, or recenter a contact lens.

Getting a foreign object in the eye is the most common eye problem associated with riding. Fortunately, these foreign objects are usually in the form of minor irritants, such as dust, dirt, or sand. More serious intrusions, such as a blow to the head, may produce bleeding in or under the skin, causing a black eye. An ice pack will reduce swelling until a doctor can evaluate the injury.

Care of the Eyes

Fortunately, the eye has a number of natural protective mechanisms. It is recessed in a bony socket; the quick-blinking reflexes of the eyelids and eyelashes deflect most foreign particles; and tears wash away most minor irritants. If you do get something in your eye, follow these simple guidelines:

- Do not rub your eye or use a dirty cloth or finger to remove the obstruction.

- Irritants can often be eliminated by looking down and pulling the upper eyelid outward and down over the lower lid.

- If you see a particle floating on your eye, you may gently remove it with the corner of a clean piece of cloth.

- Apply an eyewash or tap water to flush out the irritating particle. If the object doesn't wash out, keep the eye closed, bandage lightly, and seek emergency professional care.

Whatever your recreational activity, your vision plays a vital role in helping you enjoy the sport and perform at peak efficiency. Your eyes deserve the best of care.

Wrist and Hand Injuries

Injuries to the wrists and hands are most often related to falling, although fingers can be jammed in a collision with the horse's neck. To reduce the possibility of wrist and hand injuries, follow these simple guidelines:

- Prior to riding or working around horses, remove your jewelry, especially rings and bracelets.

- Avoid riding with your fingers straight out. Keep your fingertips and knuckles curled back toward your palms, and keep your thumbs resting along the sides of your index fingers. Even when you pat your horse along the neck, keep your hands relaxed. Never lock your fingers into a stiff or rigid position.

- Avoid putting a "death grip" on your reins. Hold your reins firmly but gently. That way, if your horse should stumble, he can pull the reins through your fingers and regain his balance without hurting you.

- Gloves are a good way to protect your hands. While you ride, gloves protect your hands from the reins and weather. If you fall, gloves keep your hands from getting scratched.

Transporting Tips

To be on the safe side, riders who have suffered an upper extremity injury should be evaluated by their doctor. To safely transport a rider with an arm, wrist, or hand injury, follow these simple guidelines:

- A finger with mild swelling can be gently taped to an adjacent finger for protection. Use caution and do not wiggle the injured finger.

- An elastic bandage may be gently wrapped around an injured wrist to give the wrist support. Do not overwrap and do not pull the bandage tight.

- If possible, place a pillow in the rider's lap and allow him/her to rest the injured hand on the pillow. Do not bunch the pillow up around the injury—doing so may put added pressure on the injury.

Injuries to Arms and Legs

If the rider has a possible broken leg or arm, the best approach is not to move the leg or arm in any manner. A cold pack can be used to lessen discomfort until medical personnel arrive, and the rider should be kept warm with a blanket or covering to avoid shock. A fracture or a cracked, chipped, or broken bone can be recognized by some or all of the following conditions:

- a part of the body is bent or twisted from its normal shape;

- a bone has pierced the skin;

- swelling is severe and greater than that associated with a typical sprain or bruise;

- a hand or foot becomes extremely cold, which may indicate pinching of a major blood vessel.

Youngsters heal faster than adults, so it is important to get them prompt medical attention when a fracture occurs.

Ice and Heat Treatments

If someone falls or is stepped on by a horse, use Rest, Ice, Compression, and Elevation (RICE) to handle the injury. RICE reduces the swelling of most injuries and speeds recovery. Have the rider stop and Rest, apply Ice, Compress with an elastic bandage, and Elevate the injured arm, leg, knee, or ankle.

Ice reduces swelling and pain and should be left on the injured area until it feels uncomfortable. Remove the ice pack and rest for 15 minutes, then reapply. These are the immediate steps to take until the doctor arrives. Over the next few days, the injury should be treated with two to three 20-minute sessions per day at 2 1/2 hour intervals. This should provide noticeable improvement. Don't overdo the icing; 20 minutes is long enough. In most cases, after two or three days, or when the swelling has stopped, heat can be applied in the form of warm-water soaks. Fifteen minutes of warm soaking, along with a gradual return to motion, will speed the healing process.

Another approach to use after two or three days, and if your doctor agrees, is to begin Motion, Strength, and Alternative (MSA) exercise. The American Institute for Preventive Medicine recommends:

- Motion: Moving the injured area and reestablishing its range of motion.

- Strength: Working to increase the strength of the injured area once any inflammation begins to subside and your range of motion starts to return.

- Alternative: Regularly do an alternative exercise that does not stress the injury.

Seek the advice of a sports-medicine professional prior to starting your own treatment plan. Specially shaped pads are useful for knee and ankle injuries, and they can be used in combination with ice, compression, and elevation.

Guidelines for Reducing Injuries

Although no amount of planning and preparation can guarantee that a rider will never be injured, there are many things a rider can do individually (and a riding school, barn, or other facility can do collectively) to reduce the possibilities of injury.

- Inspect the facility and equipment for hazards. Make sure all stall, paddock, corral, and pasture fences are strong. Doors and gates should swing or slide firmly, but easily; all doors and gates should fasten securely. More injuries result from faulty equipment than from falling off a horse.

- Never leave wire, boards, logs, garden hoses, or any farm implements such as hoes, rakes, and shovels where horses can trip on them. Horses panic easily, and if they feel caught in something, their natural inclination is to pull back vigorously.

- If your barn has jumps or trail course obstacles, check them routinely to be sure that they are free from snags and loose nails. Hammer any loose nails back into place and remove any debris.

- Check the rings and pastures on a regular basis. Remove rocks and fill any holes or low places. When rings and riding trails are well maintained, a horse is far less likely to fall or have an accident. Don't wait for someone else to do it—check for yourself. If something is beyond your capacity to repair, report the hazard to the barn manager or another responsible adult.

- Personal clothing, such as jackets, coats, and sweaters, should be put in your car or tack trunk when you're not wearing them. From a horse's viewpoint, a jacket on a fence post becomes a fire-breathing dragon, and may well elicit violent behavior.

- Wear a hard hat with a chin strap whenever you ride.

- Always wear sturdy shoes or boots. Sandals and other casual footwear have no place around livestock. No matter how warm the weather, there are two good reasons to keep your feet covered: (1) going barefoot is a health hazard; and (2) the weight of a horse on your unprotected foot can cause a broken toe or an even more serious foot injury. You should realize that it's your foot that will break, not the horse's.

- For grooming and saddling, horses should be secured in cross-ties or properly tied at a hitch rail. Never tie a horse to his stall door or to the barn itself—a horse has enough strength to tear off the door and/or pull down a wall. Don't laugh; it has been known to happen. You or someone else could be badly injured in this type of accident.

- Horses should be walked with a halter and lead rope. A rope looped around a horse's neck does not give you the control you need for safety.

- Remember to warm up and stretch before you ride. If the weather is breezy or cold, keep your body covered and avoid drafts. A proper warm-up routine will reduce the possibility of a pulled muscle or other injury.

- Make sure your barn has a first aid kit, and always have fresh water available both for riders and for horses.

- Keep your voice low and avoid running, especially in barn aisles. Horses have keen hearing, and they are easily startled. Speaking softly and moving quietly greatly reduce the possibility of an accident.

- If you will be riding out on the trail, let someone know where you're going and approximately what time you'll be back at the barn. Never ride in any area where you are unsure of the footing.

- Always seek prompt medical attention for an injured rider. If you don't know what to do, call for emergency assistance immediately. Do not move an injured rider unless he/she is in immediate danger at that location. If you will have to wait long for assistance, cover the injured person with a lightweight blanket. Even a saddle blanket will do. Warmth reduces the risk of an injured person's going into shock.

10

Exercise and Physical Fitness

In any sport, your level of physical fitness greatly affects your level of performance. It is no different with riding. Top riders are top athletes, and they work as diligently at their fitness training as they do at their riding. It is a grave mistake to assume that the horse does all the work and that the rider just sits in the saddle, essentially doing nothing. Granted, the really great riders are so smooth that they give the appearance of doing nothing, but every muscle is working constantly, communicating signals and commands to the horse. Your ability to ride smoothly and effectively is directly related to your level of physical fitness. If you are flabby, winded, overweight, or otherwise out of shape, you will not be able to have that beautiful "invisible" ride.

It's never too soon, or too late, to begin exercising. Whether your riding goal is to participate in top-flight competitions or quiet, relaxing trail rides, you will be a safer, more effective rider if you get your body in good working order. Consult with your doctor before beginning any workout program. If your doctor approves of your participation, the exercises listed here are especially good for riders.

Warming Up

Regardless of your age, it's important that your body be limber and relaxed before you mount your horse. One of the best ways to limber up is to engage in gentle stretching exercises. One word of caution before you begin: Do your warm-up exercises before getting your horse out of his stall or paddock. The sight of you windmilling your arms in front of his face could cause him to bolt.

When doing riding-related exercises, your motions should be fluid. The stretching exercises should be done at a slow to medium pace, preferably in a warm environment. If there is no barn or other enclosed area where you can stretch and you must warm up outdoors, put on a jogging suit over your riding clothes and leave it on until you are ready to ride. Remember, also, to drink plenty of fluids, especially in warm weather. Your body's lymph nodes need fluid to carry away impurities. Without fluid, your circulatory system cannot function properly.

- Start with both feet on the ground, your weight balanced over the balls of your feet. Let your arms hang loosely at your sides. Wiggle your fingers, then gently shake your wrists. Now shake your arms. Rest. Tilt your chin down toward your chest and gently roll your head from side to side, eventually making a complete circle. Rest.

- Raise your arms and reach for the sky. Roll up on your toes and stretch, reaching as high as you can with one hand. Hold this position for ten seconds, then reach with the other hand and hold. Repeat this exercise five times.

- Rest your hands on your hips and, keeping your back straight and your head forward, stretch to your left. Hold. Now arch your right arm over your head so that your fingers point to your left and down. Hold. (You should feel a gentle stretch along your right side.) Do the same exercise with your left arm, fingers pointing to your right and down. Hold. Repeat this exercise five times.

- Rest your hands on your hips and bend forward from the waist. Do not bounce. Stretch gently and hold. Now, tilt your chin down toward your chest. Take your hands off your hips and let your arms hang loosely. Wiggle your fingers and shake your arms. (You should feel a gentle stretch along the backs of your legs, up through your back and neck.) Return to a standing position and rest.

- Do ten windmills with each arm, one arm at a time, forward then backward. Now work both arms together, forward then backward. Rest.

Now it's time to stretch your legs. Move to an area where you can freely swing your legs and where you will have something sturdy for support. A bar or fence post will do nicely, but watch for splinters. If necessary, wear gloves to protect your hands.

- Stand with your feet about 8-9 inches apart. Your upper torso should be balanced over your hips, your head should be up (but not tilted back), and your eyes, forward. Your body should be straight but not stiff. If you are right-handed, shift your weight to your left leg and begin the exercise with your right leg. If you are left-handed, reverse the order. (You will find your rhythm easier if you use your natural balance first.) Hold onto the bar or post with your left hand, and gently swing your right leg forward and backward 15 times. Turn around. Do the exercise 15 times swinging the opposite leg. Rest.

- Hold onto the post and balance your weight over your left leg. Stick your right leg out in front of you, toes up toward the sky, heel no more than 6 inches off the ground. Now, keeping your back straight but not stiff, push your right heel forward (not down toward the ground, forward). You should feel your calf muscle stretch. Do not bounce. Hold for a count of ten seconds, return your heel and toes to the starting position, and lower your right leg to the ground. Balance your weight equally over both feet. Rest. Repeat the exercise with the opposite leg.

Having completed your stretching exercises, you may wish to finish your warm-up with a brisk walk. If the weather is nippy, be sure to keep your muscles warm. The point of stretching is to get the blood flowing and to loosen the muscles and tendons. An untimely blast of cold air will negate your carefully executed warm-up. Keep your body warm until you are ready to ride.

Walking

Walking is fun, free, relatively painless, and one of the best general purpose exercises. Walking is so enjoyable that it doesn't really seem like exercise, yet it improves your cardiovascular fitness, circulation, breathing, leg and back muscles, and posture. Walking can be done either as a follow-up to your stretching routine, or as an exercise in and of itself.

Be sure to wear properly fitting, shock-absorbing footwear. You need to protect your tendons, joints, muscles, and bones from undue trauma, and good walking shoes can help you do so. Your footwear need not be expensive, but it must fit right to be effective. Pay attention to your socks. Do they fit correctly, or are they too large for your feet? If your foot slides or if you have excess sock wadded up under your foot, you'll never be comfortable. Improperly fitting socks prevent your foot from correctly distributing your weight in the shoe. This, in turn, limits the shoe's ability to provide the shock absorption and protection it was designed to provide. Moreover, socks and shoes that are too loose or too tight can rub on your foot, causing painful blisters. When you put on your riding boots, blisters prevent you from stepping down in your heels the way you should, resulting in a less effective and less safe ride. Pay as much attention to your exercise footwear as you would to your riding boots. Good shoes and socks are not an expense; they are an investment in your health and well-being.

When you walk, keep your back straight and your head and eyes forward. Some people prefer to bend their elbows and hold their hands in front of their bodies; others prefer to let their arms swing from the shoulder. Your step should be vigorous and your stride, comfortable.

In the beginning, you may be most comfortable walking on flat ground. After you have increased your stamina, try adding a few gentle hills to your walking routine. Don't turn this into a mountain-climbing venture, or you'll be building the wrong muscles for riding. Remember, riders want long, elastic, sinewy muscles, not bulk. Concentrate on exercises that encourage an open, flowing range of motion.

You may discover that horseback riding itself is good overall exercise. Your coordination and balance should improve, as well as how easily you use your hands. Moreover, the confidence gained can be invaluable.

Nutrition

Good eating habits go hand-in-hand with physical fitness. A rider can be in good health without being physically fit, but a rider can't become physically fit without following a well-balanced diet that contains protein, fats, and carbohydrates in the proper amounts.

Carbohydrates are sugars and starches and come in two forms— simple and complex. The simple form, found in processed foods like candy, soft drinks, or sweet desserts, is the one to avoid. These provide only "empty" calories that may taste good momentarily, but do nothing for overall health. This is low-quality nutrition. It's not necessary to eliminate them entirely from your diet, but be selective. Sugar, in its natural form, is abundant in fresh fruit, and a better way to satisfy a sweet tooth is by eating a piece of fruit, rather than a candy bar.

The U.S. Department of Agriculture (USDA) and the Department of Health and Human Services (HHS) reissued "Dietary Guidelines for Americans" in May 2000. The guidelines suggested that

Americans ". . . limit the intake of beverages and foods that are high in added sugars." For example, a Food and Drug Administration (FDA) study, published early in 2000, reported that soda consumption per person in the United States had reached 41 gallons in 1997. This is nearly double the 1970 consumption rate of 22 gallons. A 12-ounce can of soda contains nine teaspoons of sugar, an amount that you could visualize by measuring this amount into a cup or glass. The size of soda cans and bottles has kept pace with consumption, from the standard 6.5-ounce bottle of the 1950s to today's 12-, 20-, and 64-ounce containers. As soda consumption has gone up, milk, juice, and water consumption has gone down. Despite their high calories, sodas don't contain the vitamins and minerals needed for good health, so limiting your consumption is probably a good idea.

The guidelines, as they had in the past, emphasized the importance of carbohydrates and the lesser role of protein and fats in a healthful nutrition program.

Complex carbohydrates are a nutritional best friend because they are our primary source of fuel. You'll find them in bread, vegetables of all colors (especially peas and beans), fruit, nuts, pasta, and whole grains (wheat, rice, corn, and oats). They should make up about 60 percent of your well-balanced, nutritious meals throughout the day, starting with the first one.

Breakfast should be a good solid one-third of your calorie intake for the day. If you often find you are not hungry for breakfast in the morning, try eating a light dinner; you'll have an appetite the next morning, and that should help get you on a regular meal schedule. It is a cliché, but eating breakfast will make you feel better all day. Also, there is no nutritional law that requires a "traditional" breakfast. There is nothing wrong with eating a baked potato, having a hearty soup, or eating lean meat, fish, or poultry at your first meal of the day. The important point to learn is to eat well-balanced, nutritious meals throughout the day, starting with your first one.

A Guide to Daily Food Choices

Fats, Oils, & Sweets
USE SPARINGLY

Milk, Yogurt, & Cheese Group
2-3 SERVINGS

Meat, Poultry, Fish, Dry
Beans, Eggs, & Nuts Group
2-3 SERVINGS

Vegetable Group
3-5 SERVINGS

Fruit Group
2-4 SERVINGS

SERVING
KEY
☐ - minimum serving

■ - above minimum
serving guidelines

Bread, Cereal, Rice, & Pasta Group
6-11 SERVINGS

Source: U.S. Department of Agriculture and the
U.S. Department of Health and Human Services

Protein is found in many foods—nuts, dairy products, and lean meats, poultry, and low-fat fish. You don't need a 16-ounce steak every day to "build muscle." In fact, that's probably too much protein for your body to absorb efficiently; the rest just goes to waste. Try to keep your protein consumption to about 20 percent of what you eat each day, and you'll consume enough to build muscle, maintain it, and repair it when necessary.

A word on liquids: Avoid cola drinks, coffee, and tea. They are filled with caffeine and act as diuretics to take water from your body. The one liquid you should not avoid is water, which is 60 percent of your body's weight and is needed to lubricate your joints and maintain body temperature. Water is also the transportation system for the nutrients you need to stay healthy, so don't neglect this crucial liquid. One to two quarts per day will keep your body well-lubricated and prevent dehydration.

The guidelines also make statements about exercise and sodium (salt) in the diet. For the first time, Americans are urged to include "moderate daily exercise" of at least 30 minutes per day in their lifestyles and to "choose and prepare foods with less salt." This means avoiding soy sauce, ketchup, mustard, pickles, and olives.

Finally, there are no "miracle foods" or "miracle diets" or "miracle pills" that will keep you in perfect health and physically fit. A well-balanced diet, paired with regular exercise, will keep you fit for life.

Precautions

Drugs of some type have been used by many athletes for many years. We don't expect this from Olympic-class competitors, but we know it is true. One reason given for taking drugs is to win medals. Perhaps that is why they have been misnamed "performance enhancing," when in reality they are not. Steroids, amphetamines, hormones, human growth hormone (hGH), and erythropoietin (EPO) are a few drugs specifically banned by the International Olympic Committee (IOC). Steroids (anabolic-androgenic steroids, or AAS) are another drug danger, with terrible consequences for the user. Steroid use by males can result in breast development, hair loss, and acne, plus yellow skin and eyes. Among females, breasts shrink, hair grows on the face, and menstrual cycles can become irregular. For both, the result of steroid use can be permanent stunting of body growth.

The food additive androstenedione, or "andro," has been identified as a steroid and is now illegal without medical reasons. On their own initiative, the IOC, the National Football League (NFL), the National Collegiate Athletic Association (NCAA), and other sports organizations have already banned its use by athletes.

The psychological effects of steroid use are just as devastating, according to the American Sports Education Institute, which has noted the following: "Wide mood swings ranging from periods of violent, even homicidal, episodes known as 'roid rages' to depression, paranoid jealousy, extreme irritability, delusions, and impaired judgment."

The American Medical Association, the International Olympic Committee, the National Collegiate Athletic Association, and the National Football League have deplored the use of steroids for muscle building or improving athletic performance.

The negative impacts on an athlete's health of using EPO, for example, can range from sterility to increased risk of heart attack, liver and kidney disease, and some cancers. These are permanent, not temporary, health problems. EPO has caused deaths in athletes, as have amphetamines, and no one knows the long-term effects on a normal-size person of using human growth hormone.

A partial list of the consequences of taking any of these drugs follows:

- Creatine: The side effects are dizziness, diarrhea, and cramps.

- EPO: Forces the heart to work harder. Can cause heart attacks, strokes, and sudden death.

- Anabolic steroids: Higher cholesterol, "roid rages," perhaps liver disease and cancer, heart disease, and brain tumors. For women, hair on the face, lost hair from the head, acne, breast shrinkage, and cessation of menstrual periods.

- Cyproterone acetate: Stops sexual development in women.

- hGH: The side effects are unusual bone growth (or acromegaly). The forehead, cheeks, jaw, hands, and feet grow grotesquely.

- Amphetamines: Temporary boosters that increase heart rate, blood pressure, and respiration. They do not boost performance levels; in fact, they actually decrease them.

Currently, nearly 12.5 million Americans use illegal drugs, and teenagers are the fastest-growing portion of first-time, illegal drug users. The message Americans need to hear is that drugs are illegal, addictive, dangerous, unhealthy, and wrong. Teens know that drugs are the most important problem they face—before violence, sex issues, and getting into college. Drug-prevention materials for young people and adults are available by calling the U.S. Department of Health and Human Services at this toll-free number:

1-800-729-6686

Note: This book is in no way intended to be a substitute for the medical advice of a personal physician. We advise and encourage the reader to consult with his/her physician before beginning this or any other weight management, exercise, or fitness program. The authors and the publisher disclaim any liability or loss, personal or otherwise, resulting from the suggestions in this book.

11

Riding Basics

Good horsemanship is an art. No one, no matter how famous, ever learned to ride overnight. Riding well requires many years of practice and experience. Even top riders such as Olympic and World Cup competitors know that no matter how many blue ribbons they've won, every time they get on a horse, they are learning. These riders know that effective riding requires communication and harmony between horse and rider, and communication is a two-way street. Intelligent riders allow every horse they ride to communicate its feelings to them. This is not an idle exercise. What the rider learns from the horse enables the rider to bring out the horse's best performance.

Even if you are a beginner, it's not too soon to learn this valuable lesson. Whenever you approach your horse, pay attention not only to his physical condition but to his mental state as well. Does he seem a little nervous today? Perhaps you should turn him out for 15-20 minutes before you ride. Does he seem a little sluggish? Perhaps a trail ride would help. Does he shy at some particular spot in the ring? Maybe something is catching his eye that usually isn't there. Investigate these things and act on them accordingly.

Letting your horse communicate with you is not the same as letting him get away with bad behavior. The former enables you to be an active, effective horseman; the latter makes you a passenger on an unhappy ship. You maintain the upper hand by having more than one way to solve a problem. For example, let's say your horse is acting a little sluggish. You know your horse is in good health, but today he's moving like a sleepwalker. One way to solve that problem in an effective, productive manner is to go out for a trail ride. It's amazing what a trail ride can do to perk up a sluggish horse. In no time at all, your horse will feel revitalized and move forward with energy and impulsion. Now that you have maintained the upper hand by identifying the problem and coming up with an effective, productive solution, you can return to the stable and continue your ride as planned. Top riders know that looking, listening, and responding appropriately always works to the rider's advantage.

Tacking Up

After you've given your horse a good grooming, you're ready to put on the saddle, bridle, and any additional equipment. This procedure is known as *tacking up*. If your horse wears boots or bandages, put those on first. If you use a martingale or breastplate, put it around the horse's neck, then reattach the cross-ties to the halter.

The saddle is put on from the left side. Lift it over the horse's back and gently place it just above the withers. Now, slide it back toward the tail until it lies slightly behind the withers. You will feel the saddle nestle into place. If you go back too far, lift the saddle and repeat the procedure. Never pull it forward, as this would cause the hair to lie in the wrong direction. Make sure the saddle pad is not bunched or twisted. The pad should fit up into the gullet of the saddle; it should not be pulled tight across the horse's spine. If the pad isn't right, start over. Don't fret if you have to do this a few times; you will soon get the hang of it. Never mount up if the pad and/or saddle are not properly adjusted. Ill-fitting tack can give a horse a sore back.

Photo: Betty Skipper for USPC

A young rider adjusts his saddle and girth before mounting.

Once the saddle is correctly seated, reach under the horse's belly and pick up the girth (it will be hanging from the billet straps on the right side of the saddle). Make sure it hangs straight and is not looped over a post or other object. Pull it toward you. (If you are using a martingale or breastplate, run the girth through the loops.) Now, buckle the girth to the billet straps on the left side of the saddle. Leave the irons run up until you are ready to mount.

To put on the bridle, stand on the left side of the horse's head. Unbuckle the halter, slip it off the horse's face, and rebuckle it loosely around the neck. Holding the bridle by the crownpiece, lay the reins over the horse's head. This serves two purposes: (1) it gives you some control should the horse start to walk away; and (2) it prevents the horse from getting his feet and legs tangled in the reins. Next, hold the cavesson and crownpiece in your right hand; with your left, slip the bit into the horse's mouth. Secure the crownpiece over the ears, left ear first, then right ear. Pull the horse's forelock out of the browband. If necessary, adjust the cheekpieces so that the bridle fits comfortably. Fasten the throatlatch. If you are using a standing martingale, loop it through the cavesson before fastening the cavesson. Fasten any additional tack, such as a dropped noseband or a curb chain (make sure all links lie flat). Unbuckle snaffle reins, loop them through the rings of your running martingale, and rebuckle.

If you must turn away from your horse for any reason, such as to put on your riding boots or lock your tack box, put the halter on over the bridle and attach cross-ties to the halter. Never attach cross-ties directly to the bridle. For the safety of you and the horse, ask your instructor to check that everything is properly adjusted.

Mounting and Dismounting

If you're not already wearing your hard hat, put it on and fasten the chin strap. Release the horse from the cross-ties, lift the reins over his head, and lead him to the mounting block. If your barn doesn't have a mounting block, lead him into the ring and close the gate. Lead the horse from his left side. Hold the middle (buckle) of the reins in your left hand and place your right hand 8-12 inches from the bit. Look toward the direction you are moving, walk smartly, and allow the horse to follow you. Do not look at the horse, as this only encourages him to stop. Your assistant should go with you.

When you have reached the mounting area, pull your irons down and put the reins back over the horse's head. Check the girth

Photo: Gary R. Coppage for USPC

Pony Club members demonstrate how to lead a pony or horse.

and tighten, if necessary. Your assistant should stand on the right side of the horse and take hold of the bridle. You should stand on the left side, close to the saddle. Gather the reins in your left hand. Turn slightly toward the tail, and, with your right hand, turn the iron toward you. Place your left foot in the iron, resting your toe on the girth. Grasp the cantle (back) of the saddle with your right hand, grasp the mane with your left hand (don't drop the reins), and push off with your right foot. Swing your right leg up and over, taking care not to kick or gouge the horse in any way. Sink gently into the saddle—do not flop down like a lead balloon. Adjust your feet in the irons and gather the reins in both hands. When you feel secure, ask your assistant to release the bridle and step away from the horse. You are now ready to ride.

To dismount, have your assistant hold the bridle from the right side of the horse. Place the reins in your left hand and push down on the horse's neck with your right hand. Take your right foot out of the iron and swing it up and over the horse, behind you. Slide your right hand to the cantle (back) of the saddle, balance yourself a moment as you slip your left foot out of its iron, and drop gently to the ground. Push yourself slightly away from the horse as you drop. Continue to hold the reins in your left hand as you dismount, or your horse will be loose and could walk away. Should you accidentally drop the reins, your assistant can hold the horse until you regain control.

Before returning to the grooming area, run the irons up the stirrup leathers and lift the reins over the horse's neck. Lead as discussed above.

Stretching and Balancing

Stretching exercises done while mounted are very beneficial to a novice rider. They improve suppleness and balance, and increase a rider's sense of security and self-confidence. Beginner riders of any age should have a knowledgeable assistant hold the horse while the rider performs the exercises. Begin the exercises with the horse standing still.

- Sit in the center of your saddle, grasp the pommel (front) with your hands, and stretch your toes toward the ground. Now stretch your heels toward the ground. Repeat. Without rising from your saddle, stretch your upper body toward the sky as you stretch your legs toward the ground. Visualize yourself as a rubber band, stretching upward from your waist and downward from below your waist.

- When you feel secure, remove your hands from the pommel and place them on your hips. Repeat the toe and heel stretching as you slowly raise your arms out to your sides. If you start to feel insecure, lower your arms, get organized, and try again. Your goal is to raise your arms over your head while your legs are stretching down, down, down.

- Extend your arms over your head and wiggle your fingers. Now pretend you are climbing a ladder, stretching one arm higher, then the other. In your waist, you will feel your body shift gently from side to side. Your goal is to keep your seat level in the saddle as your upper body stretches from side to side. This exercise improves suppleness, and suppleness is what enables a rider to follow the motion of the horse.

- Place your hands on the pommel again. Keep your legs straight and push your heels down. Now move your left leg forward, toward the horse's shoulder. Hold onto the pommel so you don't tip backward. Return the left leg to its normal position and move the right leg forward. Alternate and repeat. When you feel confident, try moving both legs forward at the same time.

- Hold onto the pommel and swing one leg forward toward the horse's shoulder as the other swings back toward the tail. Be careful not to kick the horse. Your legs should slide smoothly along the horse's sides. For this exercise you may find it helpful to place one hand on the cantle (back) of your saddle and keep one hand on the pommel. Alternate hands. Your goal is to keep your back straight and your seat bones in contact with your saddle.

- Place your hands on your hips and face straight ahead. With your back straight, bend forward at the waist. How far can you go? Don't let your legs swing back behind you. Your goal is to be flexible in your upper body while keeping your lower body quiet and stationary. Return to an upright position. Get organized; now lean backward. If you feel insecure, hold onto the pommel and try again. Repeat. Take your time. This is a stretching exercise; speed is not the objective.

- Repeat the above exercise, but this time stretch your arms out in front of you and try to touch your horse's ears. Stretch your arms behind you and try to touch his tail. Return to an upright position. Stretch one arm forward over the horse's mane, the other behind you toward the tail. Alternate and repeat. Your goal is to develop a supple waist, a relaxed back, and a secure seat.

When you feel confident doing these exercises at a standstill, ask your assistant to lead the horse at a walk. Repeat the exercises while the horse is walking, starting with whichever one is easiest for you. If you lose your balance, ask your assistant to stop the horse immediately. If you're not too tired, reorganize and try it again; however, if you're not used to riding, your body may be telling you it has had enough. Do only what feels comfortable, and save the remaining exercises for another day.

Photo: Dawn Johnson for USPC

A helpful assistant makes learning to ride easier and more fun.

Aids

Aids are the various ways you communicate with your horse. Specifically, using aids means using your hands, legs, voice, and weight (or position in the saddle) to tell your horse what to do: start, stop, turn, speed up, or slow down. At first, using the aids will be obvious, but with practice and experience, you and your horse will move together with precision and harmony. These are your natural aids. Artificial aids include different kinds of equipment—a crop or spurs, for example.

Walking

After you have warmed up with a few stretching exercises, sit in the center of your saddle and place your feet in the irons. Before you walk forward, glance down. You should not see your toes. If you do, your feet are too far out in front of you. Roll forward onto your seat bones and bring your lower leg back underneath you. Do not rest your weight on your derriere. You are riding a horse, not an easy chair. Sit tall and push your heels down.

Gather your reins so that there is a slight loop between the bit and your hands. If you start to fall back in the saddle, the loop will prevent you from catching the horse in the mouth. Don't worry right now about your hands; their time will come. As a beginner, your primary objective is to develop a secure seat.

Gently squeeze your legs against the horse's sides. Do not kick, and keep your heels down. As the horse walks forward, relax and allow your body to follow along. If you brace against the motion, you are telling the horse to stop.

Walk along the perimeter of the riding arena. When you have made one complete circuit, ask the horse to stop. Brace your back, close your legs gently along the horse's sides (so that he steps forward into the bit), and close your fingers on the reins. If necessary, say "whoa" in a soft voice. Do not pull on the reins. If the horse fails to stop, don't get excited; simply try it again. Spend several days going from halt to walk to halt before moving on to the trot. Your horse needs time to understand you, and you need time to develop your seat.

Trotting

Because the trot has a more vigorous up-and-down motion, it is easier to learn to ride this gait when the horse is controlled by another person. Your riding instructor or assistant will stand in the middle of the ring and control the horse via the *lunge line*. One end of the lunge line is attached to the horse's bridle; the other is held by the groundperson. The horse moves comfortably in a controlled 30-foot circle. The rider does not have to steer and is free to concentrate on learning to ride.

Place your reins in your weak hand and grasp the pommel firmly with your strong hand. Squeeze your legs a bit more vigorously than before. As the horse starts to trot, pull yourself up and slightly forward, then gently return to your normal seated position. At a trot, a horse moves his legs in diagonal pairs. As one pair reaches forward, the other pair is planted on the ground. The sequence reverses with the next step; the legs that were on the ground now reach forward.

At the trot, the rider rises from the saddle on one sequence and sits on the next. This sequence of rising and falling is known as *posting*. A rider posts either on the left diagonal or the right diagonal. You are posting on the left diagonal when you rise as the left foreleg reaches forward. You are posting on the right diagonal when you rise as the right foreleg reaches forward. Don't worry about right and left diagonals just now. Concentrate on finding and maintaining a rhythm. Rise, sit; rise, sit; rise, sit. Hold your upper body erect and lean forward from the waist. If you need help, grasp the pommel and pull yourself out of the saddle. Count one-two, one-two. Keep your heels down and your shoulders back. Don't get discouraged; it takes time to master the trot.

Cantering

Many riders, even beginners, believe the canter is the smoothest of all gaits. Because the canter is a three-beat gait, the horse's lifting motion is smooth and gradual, thereby producing that wonderful "rocking chair" effect for which the canter is famous. It's best to begin on the lunge line. Concentrate on your riding and let the groundperson control the horse.

The stretching exercises you did to loosen your body will prove most beneficial. In the canter, a rider's seat bones remain in contact with the saddle, and the horse's motion is absorbed through the rider's lower back. To achieve this, the head and shoulders must remain stationary. If they tip forward, your balance will be compromised and you'll find yourself gripping with your calves. This is wrong. Your legs should lie gently along the girth, and contact should be evenly distributed between your thighs, knees, and lower legs.

Glance down to see that your toes are not visible. If they are, roll up onto your seat bones and get your lower legs back where they belong. Push your heels down. Low heels will help anchor your seat and keep your legs in the proper position.

Do not worry about your hands right now. Work from the lunge line until you perfect your balance, rhythm, and timing. Concentrate on keeping your legs underneath you, your heels down, and your seat bones in the saddle. Let your lower back become loose and supple, and keep your shoulders straight. Do your stretching and balancing exercises at least twice a week, and practice posting the trot for at least five minutes every time you ride.

Photo: Gary R. Coppage for USPC

Preparation and hard work ideally pay off in a happy, obedient horse and a textbook-perfect ride.

After Your Ride

When you have finished riding, dismount, run up your irons so they don't catch on anything, lift the reins over your horse's head, and walk him back to the cross-ties. Put the lead rope around the horse's neck and remove the bridle. Slip the halter on, fasten, and secure the cross-ties to the halter, one on either side.

Unbuckle the girth, disengage martingale or breastplate straps, and remove the saddle. Slip the martingale or breastplate over the horse's head and reattach the cross-tie.

Finally, remove any boots or bandages. If the horse is warm, walk him until he's cool. Return to the cross-ties. Clean and paint the hooves. Groom the horse thoroughly, then put him away. Feed the horse and refill the water tubs. Wash and dry the bit. Put away all tack and horse clothing.

12

Glossary

Like all sports, equestrian has a lexicon of its own. Being familiar with the language will help you understand the sport and make you a better horseman or horsewoman. Using official terms to phrase a question or explain a situation will facilitate your communication with instructors, veterinarians, blacksmiths, tack and feed dealers, and horse show officials.

AHSA American Horse Shows Association, the governing body of equestrian events in the United States. The AHSA provides rules and regulations for more than 2600 equestrian competitions each year, and serves as the official link for equestrian sports to the United States Olympic Committee as well as the world governing body of equestrian sports, the FEI (see below). Other U.S. equestrian organizations can be AHSA affiliate members and establish their own rules, so long as those rules do not conflict with those of the AHSA.

Aid a signal used by a rider to give instructions and directions to the horse. Aids are further divided into two categories: *artificial* and *natural* (see below).

Anvil   a heavy iron block with a smooth face, usually of steel, on which horseshoes are shaped.

Artificial Aid   any piece of equipment, such as crop, spurs, or martingale, that the rider employs to help convey instructions to the horse.

Automatic Timer   an electrical apparatus used for show jumping and other timed events. The horse breaks an electronic ray as it starts, triggering the mechanism that activates the clock. At the finish area, the horse breaks another electronic ray that stops the clock.

Barrel   that part of the horse's body between the forearms and the loins.

Bay   a dark-skinned horse with a black mane and tail, and normally black markings on the legs. Bays' coats range in color from yellowish-brown (golden bay), to a deep mahogany red (bloodbay), to a dark blackish-brown (seal bay or seal brown).

Bit   a device, usually made of metal or rubber, attached to the headstall and reins, and placed in the horse's mouth. The bit helps the rider regulate the position of the horse's head and is one aid used to control pace and direction.

Black   a dark-skinned horse with a black coat, mane, and tail. No other color may be present. White markings on the legs and/or face are common.

Blacksmith   a trained professional who trims and shoes horses, also known as a horseshoer or farrier. "Blacksmith" is an old term that originally applied to any artisan whose medium was iron.

Body Brush   used to remove dust from a horse's coat.

Bran   a by-product from milling grain. Wheat and oat bran are the most common types of bran used for horse feed. Served dry, bran helps to control diarrhea (see *Bran Mash*).

Bran Mash   made by pouring boiling water over a bucket of bran and allowing it to soak. Add salt and a tablespoon of brewer's yeast. Stir and serve warm. When served damp, it acts as a laxative and aids digestion. A good evening meal for tired or stressed horses (see *Bran*).

Breastplate   a device, usually of leather, that fits around the chest and attaches to the saddle and the girth. Used to prevent the saddle from slipping backwards.

Bridle   that part of a horse's tack that includes the headstall, bit, and reins.

Browband   that part of the headstall that lies across the horse's forehead, below the ears. It prevents the bridle from slipping backward.

Brush Box   a fence used in hunter and equitation classes. It can also be used in jumper classes, but is then usually enhanced by posts and rails, making for a more difficult fence.

Canter   a three-beat gait, faster than a trot, but slower than a gallop.

Cavalletti   a series of small jumps used in the basic training of a horse to encourage it to lengthen its stride, improve its balance, and strengthen its muscles. The cavalletti is also used to teach novice riders how to jump.

Cavesson   that part of the headstall that goes around the horse's nose. Also called a noseband.

CCI   international three-day event.

Cheekpiece   (1) that part of the bridle to which the bit is attached at one end and the crownpiece at the other; every bridle has two cheekpieces, one on either side. (2) Sidepieces of a bit to which the reins are attached.

Chestnut   a horse with a gold to dark reddish-brown coat, usually with matching mane and tail. Some chestnuts have a flaxen-colored mane and tail. On no account can the mane and/or tail be black. That would make the horse a bay, not a chestnut.

Clear Round   a show jumping or cross-country round that is completed without incurring any jumping faults or time faults.

Colic   an abdominal distress, often caused by an obstruction in the digestive tract. It can be very serious. Consult veterinarian immediately. Follow his/her directions regarding care and treatment.

Collection   shortening the pace by using a light rein contact and gentle pressure from the legs. Collection helps the horse find its balance by teaching it to bring the hind legs well forward, thereby supporting its body.

Colt   a male horse less than four years old.

Combination   an obstacle consisting of two or more separate elements that are numbered but judged as one obstacle. Combinations usually allow only one or two strides between elements.

Combined Training a comprehensive test of horse and rider covering three phases: dressage, cross-country, and stadium jumping; held over a period of one, two, or three days, depending on the level of difficulty.

Contact the link between the rider's hands and the horse's mouth made through the reins.

Crownpiece that part of the headstall that fits over the top of the horse's head, behind the ears.

CSIO official international jumping event.

CSI-W international jumping World Cup.

Curb Bit a bit designed so that, when the rider applies pressure to the reins, the shanks of the bit swivel, thereby tightening the curb chain and exerting pressure on the poll. The horse drops his head to release the pressure.

Curb Chain a lightweight chain of flat rings, fitted to each side of a pelham or curb bit. It increases leverage and control.

Curry Comb a comb made of rubber or metal. It's used primarily to clean bristles on the body brush. Metal combs should not be used on a horse. Rubber combs may be used in a circular motion on the shoulders, neck, and hindquarters.

Dam the female parent of any horse or pony (see *Sire*).

Dandy Brush stiff-bristled brush used to remove mud.

Double Bridle a bridle consisting of two separate bits, a snaffle and a curb. Bits may be operated independently for maximum effect.

Dressage the art of horse and rider working in complete harmony to perform all movements in a balanced, supple, and obedient manner.

Equine (1) a horse; (2) of, or pertaining to, a horse.

Eventing (see *Combined Training*).

Farrier a person who trims and shoes horses (see *Blacksmith*).

Fault a method of scoring errors such as knockdowns, refusals, or time penalties.

FEI the *Fédération Equestre Internationale* (International Equestrian Federation), the governing body of international equestrian events, including the Olympics and World Cup. All national federations must comply with the rules of the FEI during international competitions.

Fence refers to an obstacle to be jumped in a horse show or on a cross-country course.

Filly a female horse less than four years old.

Floating filing sharp points off the back teeth of an adult horse.

Foal a baby horse of either gender.

Forelock the long hair on top of the horse's head that hangs in front of the ears (see *Mane*).

Forge   a device for heating horseshoes so that the metal can be shaped to fit the hoof.

Frog   located on the bottom of the foot. It aids circulation to the foot and leg, and improves traction.

Gelding   a castrated male horse, incapable of breeding.

Girth   a device passed under the belly and buckled to both sides of the saddle to hold it in place.

Grand Prix   literally, grand prize. A sport performed at its most difficult level.

Gray   a dark-skinned horse with a coat of black and white hairs mixed together, the whiter ones becoming more predominant with age.

Green   a horse that has not completed its training.

Groom   (1) any person responsible for looking after a horse; (2) to clean and care for a horse.

Gymkhana   a horse show where games—egg races, relays, spoon races, barrel races, etc.—are played while on horseback.

Hackamore   a bitless bridle of two types: mechanical or bosal. On the mechanical type, reins attach to the shanks extending from the cavesson; on the bosal type, reins attach directly to the back of the cavesson.

Halter   a headpiece, to which a rope can be attached, for leading or tying a horse.

Hand   a linear measurement of 4 inches (10.2 cm). Used in measuring the height of a horse from the ground to the withers, the fractions expressed in inches, *e.g.*, a horse measuring 65 inches is 16 hands, 1 inch; written as 16.1 hands.

Headstall the parts of a bridle that fit around the horse's head and face.

Hoof the entire foot of a horse.

Hoof Pick a hooked metal device used for removing stones and debris from a hoof.

Horse Show a competition to test the qualities and capabilities of horses and riders.

Hunter a horse that competes over fences or carries a rider in the hunt field. Show hunters are judged on performance, manners, way of going, style of jumping, and (in some classes) conformation. Hunter classes are not judged on time (see *Jumper*).

Irons (see *Stirrup Iron*).

Jumper a horse that competes over fences. Jumpers are judged on their ability to clear the obstacles and (in certain classes) judged on time. They are not judged on how they look or behave (see *Hunter*).

Jump-off in show jumping, a round held to decide the winner among competitors tied for first place after the previous round. The jump-off course is usually shorter and also judged on time. The horse with the least number of faults and the fastest time wins.

Kimberwick   a bit in which a single pair of reins controls the mouthpiece; unlike a snaffle, a Kimberwick has a curb chain.

Kur   an original composition of movement performed with musical accompaniment.

Lead Rope   a cotton, leather, or nylon rope with a clip at one end for attaching to the halter. It's used for leading or tying a horse.

Liverpool   a body of water beneath an oxer or in front of a vertical.

Lunge Line   a cotton or nylon rope, 25-35 feet long. It attaches to the halter and is used to exercise the horse. With the handler standing in one place, the horse moves in a large circle around the handler.

Maiden   a stallion, gelding, or mare that has not won a race.

Mane   the hair along the top of a horse's neck, extending from behind the ears to the withers (see *Forelock*).

Mane/Tail Comb   long-toothed comb for cleaning and combing the mane and tail.

Mare   a female horse four years of age or older.

Martingale   a device that attaches to the girth at one end and either the cavesson (standing martingale) or the reins (running martingale) at the other end. It helps the rider control and balance the horse.

MSA   acronym for Motion, Strength, and Alternative exercise. One option for handling an injury.

Muck Out   to clean and remove soiled bedding from a horse's stall.

Mustang   a wild horse.

Natural Aids   the rider's body, hands, legs, and voice, all of which are used to give instructions and directions to the horse.

Near Side   the left side of a horse's body. A rider usually mounts and dismounts from the near side.

Noseband   (see *Cavesson*).

Off Side   the right side of a horse's body.

Oxer   a fence composed of two elements, with a space in between the elements. The two elements are jumped in one single effort and scored as one fence.

Pastern   That part of the leg between the fetlock joint and the hoof. Along with tendons and ligaments, pasterns function, in part, as shock absorbers.

Pelham   a bit that combines the effects of the curb and the snaffle. The snaffle rein attaches to the top rings; the curb rein attaches to the bottom rings. The curb chain attaches to the "eye" of each shank.

Pony   an equine not exceeding 58 inches in height (14.2 hands) at the withers.

Post and Rails   a type of obstacle consisting of upright posts between which are laid horizontal rails. In jumper and equitation classes, these rails may be multicolored; in hunter classes, they must be of a solid color.

Prix des Nations literally, Prize of Nations, an international team show-jumping competition. There are four riders per team, each jumping the course twice. Show jumping is scored like golf; the lowest score wins. The best (lowest) three scores from each team are then added together, the fourth score from each team being discarded. The team with the lowest combined score wins the event.

Red Flag a marker used to denote the right-hand extremity of a course or an obstacle. It must always be passed with the red flag to the right of the horse and rider (see *White Flag*).

Red Ribbon a red-colored strip of any material tied into the tail of a horse known to kick; it's used especially in the hunt field, but should be used on any kicker ridden in the company of other horses.

Refusal stopping in front of, or passing beside, any obstacle intended to be jumped.

Rein Back at the rider's command, the horse steps backward while being ridden or driven.

Reins long, thin straps or ropes attached to the bit or cavesson (see *Hackamore*). They are used by the rider to guide and control the horse.

Ring a riding arena of any size, shape, or dimension.

Roan a horse having a black, bay, or chestnut coat with a mixture of white hairs—especially on the body and neck—that modifies the color.

Saddle a seat for a rider on horseback, made in various styles, sizes, and weights, depending on its purpose.

Saddler a person who makes, repairs, or sells equipment for horses and riders, including saddles, bridles, and boots.

School (1) an enclosed area where a horse may be trained or worked; (2) the act of training a horse toward a particular goal.

Sire the male parent of any horse or pony (see *Dam*).

Snaffle possibly the oldest form of bit. A single bar, jointed, hinged, or straight, with a ring at each end to which the reins are attached. The variations on the snaffle are endless, but all have the same general action, which is to apply gentle pressure against the corners of the horse's mouth.

Sole the bottom of the foot. The frog (see above) is located in the middle of the sole, extending from the bulbs of the heels forward, halfway to the toe.

Sound a horse free from any illness, disease, blemish, or physical defect that might impair its usefulness or ability to perform, either under saddle or in breeding. Genetic defects are considered unsoundnesses, and a stallion or mare with such defects would be classified as unsound for breeding.

Spread Fence an obstacle that is wide, *e.g.*, a "hog's back" or a water jump.

Stable Rubber a cloth of any material used for polishing a horse's coat; a cloth used for general stable maintenance.

Stallion a male horse, age four or older, suitable for breeding.

Steward an official of the horse show's governing body responsible for seeing that a competition is conducted according to the rules. In the United States, stewards are licensed by the American Horse Shows Association (see *AHSA*).

Stirrup Iron a device suspended from a saddle to support the rider's foot.

Stirrup Leather an adjustable strap by which a stirrup iron is attached to a saddle, one on each side.

Sweat Scraper a curved metal or plastic blade used to scrape water or sweat from a horse's coat.

Teeth when fully mouthed, a horse has 40 teeth: 12 incisors (6 in each jaw), 4 canines (one on each side of the upper and lower jaws); and 24 molars (6 above and 6 below on each side). Fillies and mares lack canines.

Three-Day Event (see *Combined Training*).

Throatlatch a narrow strap on the headstall that fits loosely under the horse's throat. It prevents the bridle from slipping over the head.

Thrush an inflammation of the frog (see above) characterized by rot and a foul smell. It requires cleaning the sole and treating with an anti-thrush medicine.

Time Allowed a period of time in which a rider must complete a show jumping course without incurring time faults. A rider incurs time faults at the rate of one-quarter-fault for every one second over the time allowed (see *Time Limit*).

Time Limit the maximum time in which a rider may complete a show jumping course. A rider exceeding the time limit is eliminated (see *Time Allowed*). Note the difference between *Time Allowed* and *Time Limit*.

Trot a two-beat gait in which the horse's legs move in diagonal pairs.

Unsound a horse that has any defect that makes it unable to perform its intended function (see *Sound*).

USET United States Equestrian Team. A nonprofit organization that prepares American riders and horses for international competitions, such as the Olympics and the Pan American Games.

Vertical an obstacle whereby all its component parts lie on one vertical plane.

Walk a four-beat gait. The walk should be rhythmic and energetic, with the hind legs reaching well under the horse's body.

Wall of the Hoof that part of the hoof that is visible when the foot is placed flat on the ground. It is divided into the toe, the quarters (sides), and the heel.

White Flag a marker used to denote the left-hand extremity of a course or an obstacle. It must always be passed on its right-hand side. The white flag is to the left of the horse and rider (see *Red Flag*).

Withers   the highest part of a horse's back; the area at the base of the neck.

Yearling   a horse that has passed the first January 1 of its life.

13

Olympic and Equestrian Organizations

The organization of, and participation in, the Olympic Games requires the cooperation of a number of independent organizations.

The International Olympic Committee (IOC)

The IOC is responsible for determining where the Games will be held. It is also the obligation of its membership to uphold the principles of the Olympic Ideal and Philosophy beyond any personal, religious, national or political interest. The IOC is responsible for sustaining the Olympic Movement.

The members of the IOC are individuals who act as the IOC's representatives in their respective countries, not as delegates of their countries within the IOC. The members meet once a year at the IOC Session. They retire at the end of the calendar year in which they turn 70 years old, unless they were elected before the opening of the 110th Session (December 11, 1999). In that case, they must retire at the age of 80. Members elected before

1966 are members for life. The IOC chooses and elects its members from among such persons as its nominations committee considers qualified. There are currently 113 members and 19 honorary members.

The International Olympic Committee's address is—

Chateau de Vidy, CH-1007
Lausanne, Switzerland
Tel: (41-21) 621-6111   Fax: (41-21) 621-6216
http://www.olympics.org

The National Olympic Committees

Olympic Committees have been created, with the design and objectives of the IOC, to prepare national teams to participate in the Olympic Games. Among the tasks of these committees is to promote the Olympic Movement and its principles at the national level.

The national committees work closely with the IOC in all aspects related to the Games. They are also responsible for applying the rules concerning eligibility of athletes for the Games. Today there are more than 150 national committees throughout the world.

The U.S. Olympic Committee's address is—

Olympic House
One Olympic Plaza
Colorado Springs, CO 80909-5760
Tel: (719) 632-5551   Fax: (719) 578-6216
http://www.usoc.org

Equestrian Associations

American GrandPrix Association
1301 Sixth Ave West, Suite 406
Bradenton, FL 34205
Phone: (800) 237-8924   FAX: (813) 626-5369
http://www.stadiumjumping.com/aga/index.cfm

American Horse Shows Association (AHSA)
4047 Iron Works Parkway
Lexington, KY 40511
Phone: (859) 258-2472   FAX: (859) 231-6662
http://www.ahsa.org

Intercollegiate Horse Show Association (IHSA)
PO Box 741
Stony Brook, NY 11790-0741
http://www.ihsa.com/

North American Riding for the Handicapped Association, Inc. (NARHA)
P.O. Box 33150
Denver, CO 80233
Phone: (800) 369-RIDE   FAX: (303) 252-4610
http://www.narha.org

United States Combined Training Association(USCTA)
525 Old Waterford Rd., NW
Leesburg, VA 20176
Phone: (703) 779-0440   FAX: (703) 779-0550
http://www.eventingusa.com/

United States Dressage Federation (USDF)
P.O. Box 6669
Lincoln, NE 68506-0669
Phone: (402) 434-8550   FAX: (402) 434-8570
http://www.usdf.org

United States Equestrian Team (USET)
Pottersville Road
Gladstone, NJ 07934
Phone: (908) 234-1251   FAX: (908) 234-9417
http://www.uset.org

United States Pony Clubs (USPC)
4071 Iron Works Pike
Lexington, KY 40511-8462
Phone: (859) 254-7669   FAX: (859) 233-4652
http://www.ponyclub.org

14

2000
Olympic Games

The Netherlands and Germany tied for the most medals in equestrian, with four apiece at the 2000 Summer Games in Sydney. The U.S. Equestrian Team won three medals, including the nation's first individual gold medal in eventing in 24 years.

Team Three-Day Eventing

Phase 1

The dressage test ended on the first day with the U.S. riders in fourth place with a score of 103.0 points, well behind the Australians, who led with a team total of 76.6. In second and third places were teams representing Great Britain and New Zealand. The final scores at the end of the second day of dressage had Australia maintaining its lead with 112.60 points, followed by Great Britain with 115.20, and the U.S. in third place with 125.40.

Phase 2

The cross-country saw the Australians and British maintain their leads, with New Zealand moving into third place, ahead of a strong showing by the U.S. team. Point totals at that time were 114.20, 127.0, 151.20, and 160.80 for the top four teams.

Phase 3

Before the stadium jumping began, the New Zealanders were forced to withdraw when one of the three horses the team presented for veterinary inspection failed the medical check.

When the competition was over, gold, silver, and bronze medals went to Australia (146.80 points), Great Britain (161.00), and the United States (175.80), respectively. This marked the third consecutive Olympic Games in which Australians had won the gold in this category; the veteran rider Andrew Hoy has been a member of all three teams.

Individual Three-Day Eventing

This event consisted of the same three phases—dressage, cross-country, and stadium jumping—as the Team Three-Day Event.

Phase 1

At the end of the dressage phase, American David O'Connor, riding Custom Made, was in first place with 29.0 points, ahead of a German, Marina Koehncke. In third place was Heidi Antikatzidis of Greece, representing the country where dressage began.

Phase 2

O'Connor maintained his first-place lead, riding the cross-country without penalty points. He was followed by Antikatzidis, Andrew Hoy of Australia, and Mark Todd of New Zealand.

Phase 3

The final in stadium jumping saw O'Connor gain the first individual eventing gold medal for the United States since 1976, with a point total of 34.00. Hoy (39.80) and Todd (42.00) finished with the silver and bronze medals, respectively.

Team Jumping

A team from Germany—Ludger Beerbaum, Lars Nieberg, Marcus Ehning, and Otto Becker—won the gold medal. They were followed by the teams from Switzerland and Brazil. The U.S. team finished in sixth place.

Individual Jumping

There were two rounds in this event, with the penalties for both rounds added to determine the medal winners. Because the top three riders were tied at the end of the second round, the competition was decided by a jump-off.

Jeroen Dubbeldam of the Netherlands had a perfect score—no rails knocked down—and won the gold. The silver went to Albert Voorn, also of the Netherlands, and Khaled Al Eid of Saudi Arabia won the bronze. Voorn and Al Eid each knocked down one rail during the jump-off, but Voorn had the better time.

Margie Goldstein Engle, who placed highest among the American riders, finished in a tie for tenth place.

Team Dressage

This two-day event ended with the German team of Isabell Werth, Nadine Capellmann, Ulla Salzgeber, and Alexandra Simons de Ridder winning the gold. The Dutch team of Ellen Bontje, Anky van Grunsven, Arjen Teeuwissen, and Coby van Baalen captured the silver medal, and the U.S. team of Susan Blinks, Robert Dover, Guenter Seidel, and Christine Traurig took the bronze.

Individual Dressage

Anky van Grunsven of the Netherlands won the gold medal in this event, followed by two Germans, Isabell Werth and Ulla Salzgeber, who earned the silver and bronze medals, respectively. Among the U.S. riders, Susan Blinks finished eighth on Flim Flam, and Christine Traurig eleventh on Etienne.